Studying Psychology
in the United States

Expert Guidance for International Students

Edited by

Nadia T. Hasan

Nadya A. Fouad

Carol Williams-Nickelson

D0839437

American Psychological Association

Washington, DC

Published by
American Psychological Association
750 First Street, NE
Washington, DC 20002
www.apa.org

To order
APA Order Department
P.O. Box 92984
Washington, DC 20090-2984
Tel: (800) 374-2721; Direct: (202) 336-5510
Fax: (202) 336-5502; TDD/TTY: (202) 336-6123
Online: www.apa.org/books/
E-mail: order@apa.org

In the U.K., Europe, Africa, and the Middle East, copies may be ordered from
American Psychological Association
3 Henrietta Street
Covent Garden, London
WC2E 8LU England

Typeset in Meridien by Stephen McDougal, Mechanicsville, MD

Printer: Victor Graphics, Baltimore, MD
Cover Designer: Minker Design, Bethesda, MD
Technical/Production Editor: Tiffany L. Klaff

The opinions and statements published are the responsibility of the authors, and such opinions and statements do not necessarily represent the policies of the American Psychological Association.

Library of Congress Cataloging-in-Publication Data

Studying psychology in the United States : expert guidance for international students / edited by Nadia T. Hasan, Nadya A. Fouad, and Carol Williams-Nickelson.
   p. cm.
  Includes bibliographical references.
  ISBN-13: 978-1-4338-0341-3
  ISBN-10: 1-4338-0341-0
  1. Psychology—Study and teaching (Graduate)—United States. 2. Graduate students, Foreign—United States. I. Hasan, Nadia T. II. Fouad, Nadya A. III. Williams-Nickelson, Carol.

  BF.7.U6S78 2008
  150.71'173—dc22
                                     2007045485

British Library Cataloguing-in-Publication Data
A CIP record is available from the British Library.

Printed in the United States of America
First Edition

Contents

VII

INTERNATIONAL STUDENTS: TRANSITIONING TO PSYCHOLOGISTS

Contributors

Suzana G. V. H. Adams, MA, is a doctoral candidate in her 5th year of the clinical psychology program at Argosy University in Phoenix, Arizona. Her research interests include the sociocultural, educational, and psychological aspects of immigration and multicultural responsive treatment approaches for immigrants, refugees, and underprivileged children. She was born in Brazil but educated in Switzerland, France, Spain, and England. Before she immigrated to the United States, Suzana lived in Rio de Janeiro, where she managed expert aviation consultants for the Brazilian headquarters of an agency of the United Nations.

Louise Baca, PhD, is originally from Albuquerque, New Mexico. Dr. Baca received a BA from the University of New Mexico in Albuquerque. She attended Arizona State University (ASU) in Tempe and earned a doctorate in clinical/community psychology. She worked as a licensed staff psychologist at ASU's Counseling and Consultation Center for over a decade and was the assistant director of the Multicultural Advancement Program at ASU. Currently, she is a professor of clinical psychology at the Arizona School of Professional Psychology at Argosy University in Phoenix, where she specializes in creating culturally responsive therapy programs for underserved populations.

Taneisha S. Buchanan, MA, is a doctoral candidate in counseling psychology at The University of Akron in Ohio. An international student from Jamaica, she completed her undergraduate degree in psychology at the University of the West Indies in Kingston, Jamaica. Her clinical interests include health and wellness and supervision of practicum students, with research centered on understanding the experiences of ethnic minority individuals. Both her master's thesis and dissertation focus on African American women, a population with distinct experiences because of the duality of an ethnic minority and female identity.

Merry Bullock, PhD, directs the Office of International Affairs at the American Psychological Association (APA). She is deputy secretary general of the International Union of Psychological Sciences, associate editor of the *International Journal of Psychology*, and coeditor of the *Journal of Applied Developmental Psychology*. Dr. Bullock received her bachelor's degree from Brown University in 1971 and received her doctorate from the University of Pennsylvania in 1979. In addition to academic and teaching positions, she has worked at the National Science Foundation as a program officer and in the APA Science Directorate. She has lived, taught, and done research in the United States, Canada, Germany, and Estonia.

Georgia T. Chao, PhD, is an associate professor in the Eli Broad College of Business at Michigan State University in East Lansing. She received a doctorate in industrial/organizational psychology from the Pennsylvania State University in University Park. Her primary research interests are career development, organizational socialization, and international human resources development. Dr. Chao's international activities include appointments by the U.S. Department of State to represent the United States at Asia Pacific Economic Cooperation meetings and visiting professorships in Australia, China, and South Africa. Dr. Chao served on the Council of Representatives of the American Psychological Association (APA) and as chair of APA's Committee on International Relations in Psychology.

Ayşe Çiftçi, PhD, received a doctorate in counseling psychology at the University of Memphis, Tennessee, and is currently an assistant professor of counseling psychology in the Department of Educational Studies at Purdue University in West Lafayette, Indiana. She received the Ellin Bloch and Pierre Ritchie Honorary Scholarship from the American Psychological Association of Graduate Students in 2005 for a study of "The Competence Level of International Psychology Interns." Her research interests include cross-cultural psychology, immigration (with an emphasis on families), international students, and psychological well-being and coping.

Priscilla Dass-Brailsford, EdD, a native of South Africa, is a faculty member of the Division of Counseling and Psychology at Lesley University in Cambridge, Massachusetts. She has worked extensively with victims of trauma and conducted court-ordered sexual abuse evaluations. Dr. Dass-

Brailsford has several ongoing research projects on resiliency among political trauma survivors, on community violence, and on racial identity development. She has published on the topics of child abuse and neglect, resiliency, and the effects of trauma. Her first book, *A Practical Approach to Trauma: Empowering Interventions*, was published in 2007. She is cochair of the Multicultural Committee of Division 56 (Trauma Psychology) of the American Psychological Association (APA) and is a member of APA's Committee on Women in Psychology.

Louise A. Douce, PhD, is the director of the Counseling and Consultation Service and assistant vice president, student affairs, at The Ohio State University (OSU) in Columbus. She received a graduate degree in counseling psychology from the University of Minnesota in Minneapolis in 1977 and has been nationally active in studying education and training issues of psychologists. She is a past president of Division 17 (Society of Counseling Psychology) of the American Psychological Association (APA) and currently sits on the Council of Representatives of the APA and on the APA Board of Educational Affairs.

Carolyn Zerbe Enns, PhD, is a professor of psychology at Cornell College in Mount Vernon, Iowa, and is the 2006–2007 resident director of the Japan Study Program at Waseda University in Tokyo, Japan. Her scholarly interests include multicultural feminist perspectives on psychotherapy and pedagogy, feminist therapy in Japan, and identity development among international students. She is a member of the American Psychological Association (APA) Committee for International Relations in Psychology and chair of the APA International Committee for Women of Division 52 (International Psychology).

Raymond D. Fowler, PhD, is a past president of the American Psychological Association (APA; 1988) and former APA executive vice president and chief executive officer (1989–2003). He received a doctorate in clinical psychology from the Pennsylvania State University in University Park. In 1956 he joined the faculty of the University of Alabama in Tuscaloosa, where he remained until 1986, when he was appointed professor emeritus. In 2000 he received the Distinguished International Psychological Award from APA Division 52 (International Psychology) for significant contributions to global psychology. He is currently president-elect of the International Association of Applied Psychology.

Sandra M. Fowler, MS, is an intercultural consultant and trainer. She has served as the head of the U.S. Navy's intercultural program and is currently adjunct faculty for the Summer Institute for Intercultural Communication in Portland, Oregon. She is past president of the International Society for Intercultural Education, Training, and Research. She is the senior editor of *Intercultural Sourcebook: Cross-Cultural Training Methods*. She also coauthored the "Analysis of Intercultural Training Methods" chapter for the *Handbook of Cross-Cultural Training Methods*. Mrs. Fowler is currently the art coeditor for *American Psychologist*, published by the American Psychological Association.

Arpana Gupta, MEd, was born and raised in Zambia. She is a 3rd-year doctoral student in the counseling psychology program at the University of Tennessee in Knoxville. Her research interests include cultural and racial identity issues, acculturation, stereotypes and discrimination, suicide, public policy, and quantitative research methods. She is active in Divisions 17 (Society of Counseling Psychology) and 45 (Society for the Psychological Study of Ethnic Minority Issues) of the American Psychological Association and in the American Psychological Association Graduate Student Committee on Ethnic and Minority Association (APAGS–CEMA). Some of her positions include SERD–SAS liaison, SAS Region 5 region coordinator, APAGS–CEMA regional diversity coordinator, Division 45 incoming student representative, and Asian American Psychological Association student board representative.

Yuhong He, MEd, is an international student from China. She is a 3rd-year doctoral student in counseling psychology at the University of Missouri in Columbia. She received a master's degree in education and specialized in college counseling at the University of Delaware in Newark. Her research focuses on international students' career development, problem solving in Eastern cultures, Chinese women's career development, and career counseling with international women in the United States. She has extensive experience working with international students through direct individual and group counseling, consultation, programming, organizational leadership, and community service.

P. Paul Heppner, PhD, is a professor at the University of Missouri in Columbia. He has published more than 130 articles and book chapters and five books. He has given hundreds of presentations at national conferences and more than 40 invited international presentations. In addition, Dr. Heppner has served on several national and international editorial boards and was editor of *The Counseling Psychologist*, published by the American Psychological Association (APA). Dr. Heppner is a fellow of the APA and the American Psychological Society. In 2005–2006 he served as president of APA Division 17 (Society of Counseling Psychology). He has received awards for leadership, research, teaching, and promoting diversity issues and has received three Fulbright awards.

Sin-Wan Bianca Ho, BA, is an international student from Hong Kong and a 2nd-year doctoral student in the counseling psychology program at the University of Southern Mississippi in Hattiesburg. Ms. Ho is interested in counseling families and in interpersonal and play therapy. Her career aspiration is to integrate these two therapies to provide a new theoretical framework to use when working with families. Her research interests involve parenting, parent–child relationships, integrative child therapy, and cross-cultural studies.

Bong Joo Hwang, MA, is originally from South Korea and earned a bachelor's degree in Korean language and literature from Korea University in Seoul. He received a master's degree in marriage, family, and child counseling at the University of Southern California in Los Angeles. He is currently completing doctoral work in counseling psychology at Indiana University in Bloomington. He finished a predoctoral psychology internship at the University of Illinois at Urbana–Champaign and worked as a clinical fellow for 1 year at The Ohio State University's Counseling and Consultation Service in Columbus, where he currently works as a senior staff clinical therapist.

Arpana G. Inman, PhD, received her doctorate in counseling psychology from Temple University in Philadelphia, Pennsylvania. She is an assistant professor in the counseling psychology program at Lehigh University in Bethlehem, Pennsylvania. She has published in the area of South Asian identity (ethnicity, race, gender, and generational status), Asian American coping and mental health, international counseling, and multicultural competencies in supervision and training. She currently serves on the editorial boards of *The Counseling Psychologist, Cultural Diversity and Ethnic Minority Psychology, Psychotherapy,* and *Journal of Multicultural Counseling and Development.*

Olga Iof, MA, is a 1st-year doctoral student at Antioch University New England in Keene, New Hampshire. She was born in Baku, Azerbaijan. She immigrated to New York in 1997 and received her master's degree in psychology at Adelphi University in Long Island, New York. She is a behavioral specialist for Services for the Underserved in New York at a residential facility for the developmentally disabled. Her future plans include continuing work in the field of developmental disabilities, as well as helping immigrants adjust to life in the United States.

Jae Yeon Jeong, MS, was born in Seoul, South Korea. She and her family immigrated to the United States when she was 3 years old. She is a doctoral student in the counseling psychology program at the University of

Memphis in Memphis, Tennessee. Jeong received her bachelor's and master's degrees from the University of Richmond in Virginia and Northeastern University in Boston, Massachusetts, respectively. Her interests are in the areas of working with a diverse population, women's health, assessment and psychotherapy, and sexual trauma. She is currently working on her dissertation, which will investigate cultural coping as a moderator between minority status stress and psychosomatic symptoms in Asian Americans.

Defne Koraman, PhD, received a bachelor's degree in psychology from Middle East Technical University in Ankara, Turkey. She came to the United States to pursue graduate studies and received a master's degree in organizational psychology from Columbia University in New York, New York, and a doctorate in counseling psychology from New York University. She works as a psychologist at the Freedom Institute in Manhattan, New York, specializing in working with families of alcohol and drug abusing adolescents. In addition, she serves as the director of placements at Adelphi University in Garden City, New York, coordinating externship placements. Dr. Koraman also teaches at New York University and Adelphi University as an adjunct professor.

Amanda C. Kracen, MS, is a 5th-year doctoral student in counseling psychology at Virginia Commonwealth University in Richmond and specializes in international health psychology. After earning a bachelor's degree from Brown University in Providence, Rhode Island, Ms. Kracen worked as a researcher at the student counseling service at Trinity College Dublin in Ireland. Born and raised in the United States, she was delighted to recently receive Irish citizenship. Her clinical work and research focus on the health and well-being of health care professionals and how these factors affect patient care. She was a predoctoral fellow of the National Cancer Institute (2005–2007) and cochaired the Student and Early Career Committee for Division 52 (International Psychology) of the American Psychological Association (2005–2007).

Jieun Lee, MA, pursued a career in dance for 14 years in Korea before she decided to study psychology in the United States. Ms. Lee completed her bachelor's in psychology at Michigan State University in East Lansing, where she completed her senior honor's thesis research on cultural influences on the psychopathology of Korean women who had experienced stress. She is a doctoral candidate in the clinical psychology program at University of Maryland, Baltimore County and is working on her dissertation, which investigates the relationship among acculturation, Asian values, coping style, and psychological distress for East Asian American college students.

Hsiao-Wen Lo, PhD, received her doctorate in counseling psychology from the University of Oklahoma in Norman in 2004. She is a staff psychologist of the counseling and psychological services at Colgate University in Hamilton, New York. Her clinical and research interests include multicultural counseling, multicultural supervision, and identity development.

Anca Mirsu-Paun, MS, was born in Romania, where she lived until age 23. She received her doctorate in counseling psychology at the University of Florida in Gainesville and is currently a postdoctoral associate at the University of Florida Counseling Center. As an international graduate student, Anca taught three different undergraduate courses and served as a teaching assistant for nine separate courses. She is a member of Division 17 (Society of Counseling Psychology) and Division 45 (Society for the Psychological Study of Ethnic Minority Issues) of the American Psychological Association.

Yoko Mori, MS, is a graduate student in the counseling psychology program at Lehigh University in Bethlehem, Pennsylvania. She received her master's degree in psychology from Villanova University in Villanova, Pennsylvania, in 2003 and her bachelor's degree in psychology from Bethany College in Bethany, West Virginia, in 2001. Her research and professional interests include multicultural counseling and supervision, outreach programs for international students, social justice, and domestic violence issues. She is currently working on research on international students' supervision experiences.

Lan-Sze Pang, MA, is a graduate student from Hong Kong pursuing a doctoral degree in counseling psychology at Southern Illinois University at Carbondale (SIUC). She received her master's and bachelor's degrees in psychology from SIUC in 2006 and 2003, respectively. Her primary research and practice interests include bilingual counseling, cross-cultural adjustment issues, and career development of international students. Her thesis focused on the development of the International Student College Experience Scale, a culturally sensitive instrument that measures multiple areas of international students' college experiences in the United States. Her current dissertation project investigates the role of code-switching in emotional expression and autobiographical memory retrieval in the context of bilingual counseling.

Shonali C. Raney, PhD, is from Mumbai, India. She earned a master's degree in clinical psychology from Srimati Nathibai Damodar Tharkersey University in Mumbai, India, and a master's degree in community counseling and a doctorate in counseling psychology from Ball State University in Muncie, Indiana. She works full time as a senior staff clinical therapist at The Ohio State University's Counseling and Consultation Service in

Columbus. Her areas of professional interest include trauma, sexual assault, and issues concerning international students and Asian–Asian American–Pacific Islander students.

Benjamin Siankam, MS, was born in Côte d'Ivoire and raised in Cameroon. He holds a bachelor's degree in psychology from the University of Douala, Cameroon. He received a master's degree in clinical psychology from the University of the District of Columbia in Washington, DC, but was later converted to the principles and values of community psychology. He is a doctoral student in community research and action at Vanderbilt University in Nashville, Tennessee, and has worked at the American Psychological Association in their Office of Ethnic Minority Affairs in Washington, DC, and for the Department of Mental Health in Alexandria, Virginia.

Michael J. Stevens, PhD, is a professor of psychology at Illinois State University in Normal and a licensed clinical psychologist. He was the 2007 president of Division 52 (International Psychology) of the American Psychological Association, a fellow of Division 52, and received its Outstanding Mentor and Recognition awards. He is an honorary professor at The Lucian Blaga University in Sibiu, Romania, where he completed a Fulbright grant and received the doctor honoris causa degree. He has been invited to lecture in Argentina, China, Cyprus, Finland, Tajikistan, Uruguay, and Vietnam. His recent scholarship on international psychology includes the *Handbook of International Psychology* (2004) and *Toward a Global Psychology* (2007).

Yu-Wei Wang, PhD, earned a doctorate in counseling psychology from the University of Missouri—Columbia in 2004. She is an assistant professor of psychology at Southern Illinois University in Carbondale. Her research and professional interests include stress, trauma, and coping–problem solving; sexual abuse–assault recovery; and multicultural counseling and training issues. Her research articles have appeared in the *Journal of Counseling Psychology, Journal of College Student Development, Career Development Quarterly,* and *Journal of Multilingual & Multicultural Development.* In addition, she has published several book chapters on qualitative research methodology.

Danny Wedding, PhD, joined the University of Missouri—Columbia School of Medicine in 1991 as a professor of psychiatry and director of the Missouri Institute of Mental Health, a research and policy center serving the mental health community. He trained as a clinical psychologist at the University of Hawaii in Honolulu and the University of Mississippi Medical Center in Jackson. He later spent 2 years working as a health policy fellow and science policy fellow for the U.S. Congress. Dr. Wedding's research interests include international health, the portrayal of mental illness and addictions in films, and ways to alter attitudes about mental illness and substance abuse.

J. Juana Wu, MS, is a 4th-year counseling psychology doctoral student at Virginia Commonwealth University in Richmond. A Chinese national, she completed her undergraduate study in biology at the University of Science and Technology of China. After obtaining a master's degree in molecular, cellular, and developmental biology from The Ohio State University in Columbus, she made a career transition to the field of counseling psychology. Her research focuses on career development, especially with regard to its impact on both domestic and international college student adjustment. She is one of two cofounders and current president of International Students Support Group, a student organization at Virginia Commonwealth University.

Pia Zeinoun, BA, is a graduate student in clinical and counseling psychology at Illinois State University in Normal. She received a bachelor's degree from Notre Dame University in Lebanon and was awarded a Fulbright scholarship to pursue graduate studies in the United States. Currently, she is working toward completion of her thesis focusing on resilience in adults. Her interests include positive psychology, international psychology, cross-cultural research, personality disorders, psychology of music, and women's studies. She is president of the International House Student Association at Illinois State University and is a member of Division 52 (International Psychology) and Division 12 (Society of Clinical Psychology) of the American Psychological Association.

Foreword

Norman B. Anderson

The American Psychological Association (APA) has a strong and focused international agenda. APA's international goals include creating and strengthening alliances with psychological and other organizations across the globe, working with colleagues abroad to promote psychology throughout the world, and providing our students and members with resources that will help them develop a global perspective with respect to their research and practice. International psychology students studying in the United States are critical to APA—they help enrich our knowledge and understanding of psychology as an international discipline.

I applaud the American Psychological Association of Graduate Students (APAGS) for having the foresight to identify international psychology students as an important part of the American psychology community and for developing this book to provide much-needed support for this group of students. With nearly 4,000 international student affiliates, this group represents a large segment of APAGS members and the future of psychology.

Studying Psychology in the United States: Expert Guidance for International Students provides a comprehensive review of the central issues many international students face while training in the United States and offers practical, direct recommendations for managing these issues. The editors have organized the volume in a manner that walks students—and those interested in their development—through the major considerations and tasks involved in psychology graduate study in the United States.

Many variables contribute to the decision to leave one's home country, family, and social support system to come to the United States. After arriving in the United States, students are confronted with sociocultural adjustments, securing funding, managing their visas and work permits, ensuring they are making adequate academic progress, and for some, finding an internship and postdoctoral training.

After negotiating these tasks, students must then decide whether and when to return to their home country and plan their career trajectory. This book offers guidance for each of these undertakings and milestones so that students have the critical information they need to make informed decisions in areas that will have a major impact on their personal and professional lives. The editors and authors discuss these topics in a sensitive, respectful, and open manner, because the chapters are written by those who know about these issues firsthand. Every chapter is authored by at least one international psychology student and one psychologist, each of whom is a content expert in the specific area.

I commend the editors and authors for their outstanding contributions. This book is a "must-have" for all international psychology students and those who care about their development.

Acknowledgments

This book has been a collaborative effort between the American Psychological Association of Graduate Students and several other organizations and individuals. We thank the organizations that assisted in identifying potential contributors, including the Committee on International Relations in Psychology of the American Psychological Association (APA), the Special Task Group on Mentoring International Students of APA Division 17 (Society of Counseling Psychology), APA Division 52 (International Psychology), the Taiwan Psychology Network, and the International Association of Applied Psychology. We want to express our gratitude to several individuals who assisted in the earlier stages of this book. These individuals are Manbeena Sekhon, Merry Bullock, Raymond D. Fowler, P. Paul Heppner, Michael Madson, Gisela Lin, Thema Bryant-Davis, and Qutayba Abdullatif. We appreciate the contributions of those who reviewed the information in chapter 6 on obtaining visas and work permits: Michael J. Stevens, president of APA Division 52; Rebekka Lynne Reusser, academic advisor—international students; and Gretta Starik, immigration counselor, both from the Office of International Programs at The University of Akron in Ohio. Nadia Hasan thanks her coworkers and friends at the Archives of the History of American Psychology in Akron, Ohio, who encouraged her to pursue her interests and who served as her family for the past 3 years. Nadya Fouad extends love to her mother and father, M. Elisabeth Fouad and A. A. Fouad, who came to the United States as international students and stayed to create a wonderful life for their children. Carol Williams-Nickelson thanks the international students for whom this book is written, who are the future of psychology and who will undoubtedly bring richness, added strength, and depth to our profession.

INTRODUCTION

Nadia T. Hasan, Nadya A. Fouad, and Carol Williams-Nickelson

Introduction

Each year the United States attracts a large number of students from all over the world (Sam, 2001; Yeh & Inose, 2003). For the 2004 through 2005 academic year, there were approximately 565,000 international students studying in the United States. In 2004, approximately 23% of all international students worldwide were studying in the United States, making it the lead host country of international students (Bain, Luu, & Green, 2006). Some of these students have decided to pursue careers in psychology. Despite the large number of international students who choose to study in the United States, there are few resources available to them that offer guidance on negotiating their training experiences. There is even less information about negotiating the education process for specific academic areas such as psychology.

Impetus and Evolution

The lack of resources available for international students studying psychology in the United States was brought to the attention of the American Psychological Association of Graduate Students (APAGS). APAGS offers a free Web site for international student members of APAGS, APAGSINTERNATIONAL, and several members on the listserv posted questions about their training experiences. These questions ranged from how to apply to universities in the United States to how to find a job after international students have completed their education requirements. Other questions posted to the listserv included how to adjust to life in the United States, how to make friends, how to apply for internships, and questions on visa requirement clarifications. These were answered by other international students on the listserv who shared their experiences on specific topics. The listserv monitor would also consult experts within the APAGS and the American Psychological Association regarding questions that other students could not answer. Several of the listserv questions were repeated many times; thus, it was recommended that answers to common questions be recorded in an organized way so all international students could refer to these answers. Therefore, the idea of creating a resource guide for international students studying psychology in the United States was based on the needs of APAGS international student members.

Rationale and Goals

Because of the overwhelming need to address the concerns of international students studying psychology in the United States, APAGS created this comprehensive resource book to help international students throughout the training process. The topics addressed originated from the listserv discussions and from a focus group of listserv members. Several focus group members became the student contributors to chapters in this book, and expert psychologists were recruited and paired with international student contributors to address specific topics. Most chapters have both psychologist and international student contributors who have collaborated to create practical chapters about enhancing the training experiences of international students. To learn more about the contributors to this book, see the section on Contributors. The goal of this book is to address the specific concerns of psychology international students throughout the training process and to provide helpful information for faculty and other personnel (i.e., supervisors, advisors, administrators, researchers) about working with psychology international students. As this book is a practical resource for international students, all chapters focus on the applied aspects of the chapter topics, not the research theory.

Overview

This book is divided into seven parts, with 15 chapters. Part I provides an introduction to the book. Specifically, chapter 1 offers information about the definitions and demographics of international students in the United States. Part II discusses the early aspects of training related to the decision to study psychology in the United States. For instance, chapter 2 describes topics to consider before studying in the United States; chapter 3 explains the benefits and challenges of studying psychology in the United States. Part III focuses on funding resources and legal requirements to studying psychology in the United States. More specifically, chapter 4 informs readers about how to locate international student resources at the university level, and chapter 5 lists funding resources for international students. Similarly, chapter 6 provides information about visa and work permits for international students.

Furthermore, Part IV provides information about the sociocultural aspects of studying in the United States. For example, chapter 7 outlines information about culture in the United States and chapter 8 provides recommendations for international students about sharing their culture with others. Chapter 9 addresses international students' relationships with faculty and supervisors. Each chapter addresses the sociocultural adjustments that international students make when studying in the United States.

Part V contains two chapters that focus on the academic development of international students. For instance, chapter 10 describes the experiences of international students in the classroom. This includes international students who teach other students and international students who are taught by professors. More specifically, this chapter addresses cultural variations in learning and classroom structures, accent and language concerns, and teaching techniques. Chapter 11 provides recommendations for conducting research in the United States. These chapters are written to assist international students in adjusting to the classroom environment in the United States, and to help international students in completing research requirements.

Additionally, Part VI consists of two chapters that address internships, postdocs, and employment options for international students. Chapter 12 discusses the internship process for applied psychology international students studying counseling, clinical, and school psychology. Chapter 13 describes information about applying for postdocs and securing a job in the United States. These chapters are written to assist international students in getting matched to an internship site that fits their needs and in obtaining postdocs and jobs in the United States.

Furthermore, Part VII provides information for international students to transition from being graduate students to becoming psychologists. Chapter 14 provides recommendations for international students to enhance their professional development. This chapter also provides recommendations for faculty about how to increase the professional development of international students. Chapter 15 is the last chapter, and it describes the process of returning home for international students. Thus, this section concludes the training process for international students who decide to study psychology in the United States.

Finally, it is important to note that the chapters in this book vary in several ways. First, due to the paucity of research available about the experiences of international students, the chapters differ in the amount of research literature cited. Some chapters are based in the research literature; others depend heavily on the expertise of the contributors. Second, although this book is directed to international students and the individuals who work with them, some chapters are directed toward students, and others address both students and others who work with them. Last, the chapters vary in the amount of additional resources provided for the readers. Some provide additional resources by referencing books and website resources, although other chapters do not have any additional resources listed. All additional resources for this book are listed in Appendix B.

Conclusion

This book is a comprehensive, practical resource guide for international students who study psychology in the United States and the faculty and other personnel (i.e., supervisors, advisors, administrators, researchers) who work with them. This book addresses the unique concerns that psychology international students have throughout the training process. This includes information on helping students decide whether or not to study psychology in the United States and guidance in helping international students locate employment in the United States or in their country of origin. Therefore, this book is an advantageous resource to understand the training experiences and needs of psychology international students.

References

Bain, O., Luu, D. T., & Green, M. F. (2006, October). Students on the Move: The Future of International Students in the United States. *American Council on Education Network*. Retrieved January 20, 2007, from http://www.acenet.edu/AM/Template.cfm?Section=InfoCenter&CONTENTID=18573&TEMPLATE=/CM/ContentDisplay.cfm

Sam, D. L. (2001). Satisfaction with life among international students: An exploratory study. *Social Indicators Research, 53,* 315–337.

Yeh, C. J., & Inose, M. (2003). International students' reported English fluency, social support satisfaction, and social connectedness as predictors of acculturative stress. *Counselling Psychology Quarterly, 16,* 15–28.

Background Characteristics of International Students

1

In 2004, there were 2.5 million individuals studying abroad throughout the world (Bain, Luu, & Green, 2006). The United States is the leading host nation, accommodating almost one quarter (23%) of all international students in 2004; by comparison, the United Kingdom hosted 12% of these students, Germany hosted 11%, France hosted 10%, and Australia hosted 7% (Bain et al., 2006).

We begin this chapter with an overview of the definitions of this student population within the United States. Next, we present some empirical data on the demographics of this diverse group of students from different nations around the globe, including the limited available data on international psychology students. Given the limited systematic and scientific data on international psychology students in the United States, we (Pang & Bullock) developed an electronic survey in an attempt to augment the snapshot view of this specific student population. In this chapter we provide pilot data on these students' educational backgrounds, career directions, and career–academic goals upon graduation. Finally, we present the limitations of the survey study by discussing how this study should be expanded as the increasing enrollment of international students in psychology demonstrates the need for such information.

Definitions

Individuals who leave their home country and study in another country for a certain period of time have been referred to by various terms, including *foreign students* (Berry, 1985; Dunnett, 1981) and *sojourners* (Church, 1982; Nash, 1991). Because of the negative connotations associated with the word *foreign* (Pedersen, 1991), many scholars have used the term *international students* in the literature. We use this term throughout this chapter to maintain clarity and consistency. In addition to inconsistency in naming this student population, the term is not well defined (Bain et al., 2006; Wang, Lin, Pang, & Shen, 2006). There is no global agreement on the definition of an international student because of the varied immigration regulations in different countries (Bain et al., 2006).

The United States defines international students as individuals who hold a nonimmigrant student visa (i.e., F-1 or J-1) to receive undergraduate or graduate education for a temporary and restricted amount of time in the United States (Wang et al., 2006). For additional information about relevant visa regulations for international students in the United States, please refer to information in chapter 6 on visa and work permits. International students are not considered U.S. citizens, immigrants, refugees, or permanent residents (Bain et al., 2006). This definition groups international students solely by their visa status, and it may be too narrow. For example, it excludes those students who are permanent residents (i.e., carry green cards), but identify themselves as international students. Regardless of the definition, international students are a heterogeneous population in terms of geographical location, language, religious beliefs, traditions, ethnicity, and nationality (Sodowsky & Plake, 1992; Wang et al., 2006).

DEMOGRAPHICS OF INTERNATIONAL STUDENTS IN THE UNITED STATES

According to a report from the Institute of International Education, there were 564,766 international students studying in the United States in the 2005 through 2006 academic year (Gardner & Witherell, 2006). Fifty-eight percent of these students came from Asia. The top countries of origin in Asia were India (14%), China (11%), Korea (10%), and Japan (7%). Other countries sending a large number of international students to the United States included Canada, Taiwan, Hong Kong, Turkey, Pakistan, Kenya, and France. About 46% of international students were graduate students and 42% were undergraduate students. The most popular fields of study for these students were business (18%) and engineering (16%), followed by physical and life sciences (9%) and social sciences (8.2%).

INTERNATIONAL PSYCHOLOGY STUDENTS IN THE UNITED STATES

In the United States, over 8,000 international students (1.4% of the total international student population) were majoring in psychology in the

2005 through 2006 academic year, representing a slight increase of 3% from the previous year (Gardner & Witherell, 2006). According to the *Science and Engineering Indicators 2006 Report* published by the National Science Foundation (Oliver, 2006), international students made up 6% of the psychology graduate student population in the 2004 through 2005 academic year, and 13% of these students were enrolled in clinical psychology programs. The average number of full-time international students enrolled in psychology graduate programs was slightly over 500 between 2000 and 2004 (Oliver, 2006). Unfortunately, precise data on the number of psychology international students at the undergraduate and postdoctoral levels is not available, nor is detailed information about their enrollment in the different psychology graduate programs.

Little information is available about international psychology students in the United States at the graduate level because psychology graduate programs do not routinely report the enrollment percentage of international students. In addition, there aren't any existing organizations specifically for such students that would allow ready identification of international students. Because of the paucity of data on international students in psychology, we developed an electronic survey to describe background characteristics of this population. We developed survey questions from a literature review of studies on career development of international students (e.g., Spencer-Rodgers, 2001; Yang, Wong, Hwang, & Heppner, 2002). The questions on the survey asked about demographic information (e.g., place of origin, age, sex, type of visa); psychology background (e.g., where degrees were earned); reasons for studying psychology in the United States; career directions (e.g., working permanently in the United States, working permanently in homeland); and career objectives (e.g., academia, consultation). A list of the survey questions is provided in Appendix A.

Participants were recruited from the American Psychological Association of Graduate Students International Students and the Taiwan Psychology Network Listservs. Psychology students in the United States who identified themselves as international students were eligible for this pilot survey study. The pilot group contained 10 participants of undergraduate and graduate status, most of whom were women (80%). Among the graduate participants, most (90%) are from clinical and counseling psychology programs. Participants ranged in age from 22 to 37 and came from East Asia, Eastern Europe, Canada, and the Caribbean. Most respondents (60%) had studied psychology in their home country before coming to the United States.

The majority of the pilot sample was studying in the eastern United States, primarily in doctoral (PhD) programs. All respondents (i.e., undergraduate students, graduate students, and predoctoral interns) indicated receiving financial assistance (e.g., scholarships outside their programs, tuition waivers, and stipends as research assistants or teaching assistants). Respondents' reasons for studying psychology in the United States focused on the availability of better opportunities or programs than offered in their home country. At the time of the survey, half the respondents reported a desire to go into academia, and almost all (80%) planned on also having a practice. This is not surprising, given that most of the students were in counseling or clinical psychology programs. Approximately half the respondents planned to stay permanently in the United States, and half planned to return to their home country upon graduation.

Because of the small sample size, drawn from a restricted sample pool, and the pilot nature of the survey, the data of this study cannot be generalized to the diverse international psychology population in the United States. The information does, however, provide an illustration of the kind of information that would help provide psychology faculty, student peers, supervisors, administrative officers, program directors, department chairs, and administrators of student services an initial understanding of the international psychology student population. Such a survey, conducted on a broader scale by educators, administrators, and researchers, would help provide systematic and comprehensive data on the lived experiences of this specific student population.

Conclusion

The international student population studying psychology in the United States is a sizable group. Leong and Blustein (2000) predicted that as a result of the advent of multiculturalism in psychology in the last decade, enrollment of international students in applied psychology programs such as clinical, counseling, and educational psychology will continue to increase. As we discussed earlier in this chapter, international students have unique background characteristics (e.g., nonimmigrant temporary student visas) and culture-specific academic histories, career directions, and career goals. Given the lack of research on the international psychology student population in the United States, we believe that survey studies such as the one described in this chapter are important to ensure that the experiences of international psychology students can be better understood and the culture-specific academic needs of these students can be met.

References

Bain, O., Luu, D. T., & Green, M. F. (2006, October). Students on the move: The future of international students in the United States. *American Council on Education Network.* Retrieved January 20, 2007, from http://www.acenet.edu/AM/Template.cfm?Section=InfoCenter&CONTENTID=18573&TEMPLATE=/CM/ContentDisplay.cfm

Berry, J. W. (1985). Psychological adaptations of foreign students. In R. J. Samuda & A. Wolfgang (Eds.), *Intercultural counseling and assessment: Global perspectives* (pp. 235–248). Lewiston, NY: C. J. Hogrefe.

Church, A. (1982). Sojourner adjustment. *Psychological Bulletin, 91,* 540–572.

Dunnett, S. C. (1981). *Factors affecting the adaptation of foreign students in cross-cultural settings* (Special Studies Series No. 134). Buffalo: State University of New York at Buffalo, Council on International Studies.

Gardner, D., & Witherell, S. (2006). *Open door 2006: International students in the U.S.* Institute of International Education Network. Retrieved November 16, 2006, from http://opendoor.iienetwork.org/

Leong, F. T. L., & Blustein, D. L. (2000). Toward a global vision of counseling psychology. *The Counseling Psychologist, 28,* 5–9.

Nash, D. (1991). The course of sojourner adaptation: A new test of the U-curve hypothesis. *Human Organization, 50*(3), 283–286.

Oliver, J. (2006, July). First-time S&E graduate enrollment of foreign students drops for the third straight year. *National Science Foundation Network.* Retrieved January 20, 2007, from http://www.nsf.gov/statistics/infbrief/nsf06321/

Pedersen, P. B. (1991). Counseling international students. *The Counseling Psychologist, 19*(1), 10–58.

Sodowsky, G. R., & Plake, B. S. (1992). A study of acculturation differences among international people and suggestions for sensitivity to within-group differences. *Journal of Counseling & Development, 71*(1), 53–59.

Spencer-Rodgers, J. (2001). Consensual and individual stereotypic beliefs about international students among American host nationals. *International Journal of Intercultural Relations, 25,* 639–657.

Wang, Y.-W., Lin, J. C. G., Pang, L.-S., & Shen, F. C. (2006). International students from Asia. In F. T. L. Leong, A. G. Inman, A. Ebreo, L. Yang, L. M. Kinoshita, & M. Fu (Eds.), *Handbook of Asian American psychology* (2nd ed., pp. 245–261). Thousand Oaks, CA: Sage.

Yang, E., Wong, S. C., Hwang, M., & Heppner, M. J. (2002). Widening our global view: The development of career counseling services for international students. *Journal of Career Development, 28,* 203–213.

Yoon, E., & Portman, T. A. A. (2004). Critical issues of literature on counseling international students. *Journal of Multicultural Counseling and Development, 32,* 33–43.

COMING TO THE UNITED STATES ‖

Defne Koraman and Merry Bullock

Topics to Consider Before Studying in the United States

2

I n this chapter, we outline basic issues that need to be carefully considered by potential international students. The information received prior to international relocation is a significant factor affecting a student's satisfaction with quality of life issues (Sam, 2001). It is important that as a potential international student you consider issues in the following areas: admissions, financial support, housing, campus life, relationships, and degree mobility.

Issues Related to Gaining Admission

There are two major considerations in gaining admission to a graduate school in the United States. Candidates are required to complete necessary standardized tests and put together a competitive application package. We address pertinent issues surrounding these requirements in the following sections.

TESTING REQUIREMENTS

Testing requirements can be one of the most difficult aspects of the graduate school application process. The logistics of taking these tests may pose a challenge for you because the tests may not be offered frequently in your home country. Figuring out where the necessary tests are offered and how often they are given can make you even more anxious about taking the tests. As is the case with the entire application process, advanced planning and organization will help ease this anxiety. You should leave enough time in the application process to retake the exams, in the event your initial exam scores are not satisfactory. Remember, too, that all valid test scores on standardized exams are reported to universities. Because the format and content of the exams change over time, the following discussion only covers general information. You should consult the Educational Testing Service (ETS) Web site (http://www.ets.org) for more information on standardized exams such as the Graduate Record Examinations (GRE) and Test of English as a Foreign Language (TOEFL).

GRE General and GRE subject tests in psychology are often required for admission to graduate programs in psychology. If you are not a native speaker of English, you may feel apprehensive about completing the verbal reasoning section. In addition to the verbal reasoning section, candidates are evaluated on quantitative reasoning, critical thinking, and analytical writing skills. International students who participated in a qualitative study investigating perceptions toward the GRE revealed that they perceived the content and framework of the GRE to be biased against them (Mupinga & Mupinga, 2005). If you share this perception, you may feel frustrated about taking the exam.

Additionally, students who speak English as a second language will need to take the TOEFL. The TOEFL is an assessment of a person's listening skills, written expression, and reading comprehension in English (ETS, 2007b); therefore, university admissions officers use these scores to determine whether a student will be able to meet the requirements of graduate study in the United States. It is administered in Internet- (which also tests speaking abilities), computer-, and paper-based formats, depending on the location of your testing center. Please refer to the TOEFL section of the ETS Web site for further information on format, coverage, testing locations, and practice questions (see http://www.toefl.org/). Furthermore, although acceptable scores vary from school to school, they are almost always an admission requirement, so please check the minimum score requirements on your program's Web site.

It may be reassuring to know that it is possible to start and sustain a new life in the United States with a limited command of English. However, succeeding in demanding graduate programs is highly contingent on language proficiency. This is especially true for students seeking degrees in applied psychology fields such as clinical, counseling, or school psychology because a strong command of English is essential to conducting clinical work.

COMPLETING GRADUATE SCHOOL APPLICATIONS

The keys to successful completion of graduate school applications are time, organization, and perseverance. The ability to download and post applications online has made the process much friendlier for international candidates. The process may serve as a test of your organizational skills because you will need to complete application forms, create personal statements, collect letters of reference, and meet the appropriate deadlines. We highly recommend that you maintain detailed notes about application requirements and keep track of the status of your applications.

For many international candidates, choosing potential schools out of an extremely large pool of choices becomes a great challenge. The first chapter author, Defne Koraman, was one of the students facing that challenge.

> As a freshman at Middle East Technical University (Ankara, Turkey), I knew that I wanted to pursue graduate studies in the United States. However, when it was time to apply, my anxiety regarding the choice of schools was intensified by the fact that I had very limited knowledge about these schools. I did not know where most states are, had not heard of most of the schools, and did not know how to search for more information. At the time, use of the Internet was not commonplace, which made it even more difficult to find information. Fortunately, I found a book outlining graduate programs in the United States. The best plan I came up with to narrow my choices was to review potential schools with a friend with a map of the United States in hand. I eliminated western states because they were too far from home, ruled out some that did not seem interesting enough, and crossed more schools off my list for reasons that now, 13 years later, I cannot recall. The fact is that my decision-making process was purely impulsive and random. Nonetheless, we had a lot of fun that afternoon, I managed to choose excellent schools, and I felt much less anxious about the application process.

As the preceding personal example indicates, there are many ways to select potential universities. Ultimately, personal factors will influence the selection process. Some areas to investigate about programs at a particular university include the fit between your interests and those of the faculty, opportunities for research and teaching, and availability of mentoring. The selection process may also be facilitated by using such Internet resources as e-mailing other international students studying psychology in the United States and joining electronic mailing lists and online forums. Collecting first-hand information about universities and specific programs from fellow international students is an invaluable decision-making tool.

FINANCIAL CONCERNS

Graduate education in the United States is expensive, and living expenses vary by geographic location. Proof of financial ability to pay for your education is a requirement to obtain a student visa. It is important to note that it is not an option to work off campus while on an international student visa. Although difficult for many international candidates, you can secure financial funding in several ways. In this section we provide a brief review of some financing options, but please refer to chapter 5 for detailed information on funding. Some universities offer attractive, merit-based scholarships for their students. These programs are often competitive and may be difficult for international students to obtain. To increase your chances of being awarded a full scholarship package, it is important that you apply to less competitive programs. Another option is for you to work as a graduate assistant and receive funding in exchange for teaching or conducting research. You may be able to fund your studies from your country of origin. Some countries have government or private scholarships available for students willing to return to the country after completion of studies. You may also try to work a limited number of hours on campus to cover or supplement your financial resources. Regardless of the type of funding, you should complete your research and try to discover as many opportunities as possible to maximize your chances of obtaining financial funding.

Establishing a New Life in the United States

During the intense application process, some candidates postpone thinking about the details of living in the United States after admission. After you have been admitted to a program and the initial celebration ends, you will find yourself focusing on how to set up a new life in a different environment and culture. In this section, we review issues related to housing, health care, campus and community life, and relationships.

HOUSING CONCERNS

Identifying appropriate housing can be difficult for first year international students. Housing concerns have been identified as one of three major areas for which international students seek counseling (Das, Chow, & Rutherford, 1986). You may find that one convenient choice is to secure a place in university housing. The opportunity to obtain a furnished accommodation within the university community presents a sense of safety to students arriving from overseas. The added incentive to choosing university housing is that it affords many opportunities to meet fellow students, as well as easy access to on-campus events and services. However, the downside to some university residences is that living on campus costs more than finding a place to live off campus.

You may decide that finding off-campus housing is a good option. Given the high cost of living, you may find it advisable to live with roommates. Living off campus is more likely to expose you to people from different walks of life, through roommates and the local community. There are many ways to find affordable and convenient off-campus housing, including by checking local newspapers and online forums as well as using university based off-campus housing support. It is important to be cautious about whom to choose as a roommate, and it is also important to consider transportation costs to and from campus.

CAMPUS LIFE

Becoming part of a new community is an exciting process. From the university campus to the broader local community, there are many opportunities to get connected, explore, and learn. Browsing through your school's Web site before you arrive in the United States will give you a good idea of what to expect. After you have arrived on campus, it is a good idea to use the official orientation week to explore the campus, facilities, and social activities. Bulletin boards and the local campus paper are tremendous resources that can help you become aware of what is going on around campus. We recommend taking time to become comfortable with the local culture, environment, and social life before your study load becomes very demanding.

Most universities offer many valuable services, and you should use them as much as possible to enhance your new life as an international student. You might find that adjusting to life in a different country while undertaking graduate studies is very stressful, especially during the first few months. Fortunately, most schools offer many resources to help manage academic and personal life concerns. The most important resource is the international student office. You'll find that keeping in close touch with this office is not only vital to maintaining your visa status but also you will have access to advisers who are eager to help you make the most of your experience in the United States. Whether by attending their workshops or meeting with their advisors, this office is certain to provide you with valuable information.

Another terrific campus resource is the gym. Regular exercise is a valuable tool for stress management and good health. If you develop any adjustment difficulties or personal concerns, the university counseling center is an affordable or free and confidential place to obtain help. For academic concerns, you can turn to many different resources at most universities. The writing center provides valuable assistance to students by helping improve scholarly writing skills, which is an especially crucial resource for students for whom English is a second language. Most libraries have subject area reference librarians, and you will find that working closely with the psychology reference librarian will help you learn to effectively use research tools.

Life on a typical American campus is rich in terms of extracurricular activities. There is usually great diversity in the types of student organizations on campus. By joining a student organization, you will easily find people who share common interests, backgrounds, and philosophies. In addition to student organizations, there are many free events taking place around campus at any given time. You will find that attending these events is an excellent way to stay connected with people and activities and make new friends.

Beyond the campus, the international relocation experience presents a wonderful opportunity to explore a new country. The best way to discover any new city is by walking and driving to different areas of town. A good way to identify new places to explore is by reading local papers and area guides. You should practice safety precautions and be cautious of areas of town that are not safe for visitors. The international student office may be able to provide safety tips for you.

HEALTH CONCERNS

A major concern for all international students is maintaining their health and obtaining treatment for any health concerns or issues that might arise. Fortunately, most universities have excellent health care centers. All students are required to carry some type of health insurance and for most international students this means purchasing the university's health plan. In addition, to start classes you will be asked to provide proof of vaccinations and obtain a health clearance. To minimize delays and stress, you should obtain any vaccination records and prepare translations, if needed, before your arrival in the United States. Typical vaccination requirements for most universities include measles, mumps, and rubella, but you should check with your particular school for a full list of requirements.

RELATIONAL ASPECTS OF MOVING TO THE UNITED STATES

Relationships play an important part in the lives of international students and several chapters in this book address this issue in depth. In this section, we try to provide a brief overview of concerns you should take into account when planning to come to the United States.

If you come to the United States as a student and are joined by family members, you will have built-in social support; however, there are potential problem areas associated with moving family members. Spousal adjustment has long been known to be an integral part of any sojourn experience. A common area of concern is for the spouse who stays home while the husband or wife pursues graduate studies. As spouses are not permitted to work while on a dependent visa status, they often find themselves at a loss as to how to spend their time in a new setting away from family and friends. In the case of families with children, there are issues and concerns about school and adjustment to a new environment. Again, the campus community is possibly the best place to seek help for any difficulties in these areas. Whether to connect with other families in similar situations or seek advice from the international student office, you should try to make the best of the support that is already in place. Spouses might benefit from taking noncredit courses or other workshops offered on campus or elsewhere in the surrounding area, as well as making time for interests they might not previously have had the time to pursue.

Whether you are alone or accompanied by family, maintaining your relationships with people at home remains an important concern. Typical fears for international students center on the health of parents and other family members, being disconnected from friends and family, and the logistics of maintaining a close relationship with home. Fortunately, the Internet has provided a great opportunity to maintain contact with little or no cost. E-mails, Internet calls, voice over Internet protocol, and video cameras offer a world of communications from your computer. Old-fashioned letters or postcards are also wonderful ways to keep in touch with friends and family. There are many inexpensive ways to make phone calls, such as purchasing phone calling cards or signing on to an international phone plan. If you are like most international students, you will find that traveling home to see family and friends is a priority. Travel home is not only a great remedy for homesickness but also a way to reestablish contact with your loved ones. Important concerns about travel are its cost, how long you can stay at home, and time of year to travel. Depending on where your home country is located, certain travel times might be more expensive. Alternatively, you may find it less expensive to have family and friends visit you in the United States. The time to reconnect and share your new experiences with friends and family is invaluable to your success as a graduate student.

Many personal factors determine how quickly new relationships are built. A major challenge for many international students is that they have never lived in as ethnically and racially diverse environment as the United States. Stereotypes about Americans and different ethnicities in particular might inhibit you from trying to build new relationships. You may find it easy to fall into the trap of keeping to yourself, but unless you embrace opportunities to meet new people, the chances of expanding your social circle will remain limited. One pitfall for some international students is adhering too closely to making friends only within their own ethnic group. Although this is a great way to get connected at first, it makes it difficult to fully experience the cultural, religious, and ethnic diversity that study in the United States offers. In a study of Asian international students who were studying in Australia, it was found that establishing relationships with locals was a factor that fostered better psychological adjustment (Kashima & Bundoora, 2006). One reason you might be inclined to make friends within your own ethnic group is language concerns. Regardless of how high you scored on the TOEFL, it is completely different to communicate in English all the time. It is important to remember that exposure to conversational opportunities is the best way to improve your spoken English. Many people in the United States are non-native speakers of English, and most Americans are used to hearing different accents and communicating at various levels of English.

ISSUES RELATED TO DEGREE MOBILITY

It is important to consider degree mobility before studying psychology in the United States. If you intend to continue to work in the United States after graduation, your major concerns may be immigration and visa issues. If your career plans involve working outside the United States, you need to be educated about the requirements and regulations in your target countries. Although psychology is a universal discipline, one cannot assume that a psychology degree from one part of the world will have the same weight and importance or provide access to similar opportunities in another part of the world. The regulations governing who can be called a psychologist, what education is required and at what level, and how psychologists can practice vary tremendously from country to country. There is currently some regional cooperation that facilitates mobility— for example, between the United States and Canada, or between Australia and New Zealand, and mobility possibilities within the European Union are increasing. But beyond those regions, there is no formal structure that facilitates mobility among countries.

If you plan to work outside the United States after graduation, especially as a clinician, it is crucial to contact the regulating body in your target country as soon as possible after beginning your graduate studies to ensure that requirements for that country will be met. For example, in some countries internships or other supervised training need to be done in that country (in the United States, most states require that internships be completed under the supervision of a U.S. licensed psychologist). Furthermore, in some countries licensure or its equivalent as a psychologist also requires a recognized program of undergraduate as well as graduate study. If you are planning for a career in academia, specific requirements for employment within your target county's university system need to be explored.

The best place to begin to access the information for a particular country's requirements is through that country's national psychology association (see the American Psychological Association Web site's international page, http://www.apa.org/international). These organizations may also help you establish contact with psychologists in a certain country who could provide specific and detailed information. Because many psychologists consider teaching, doing research, or practicing psychology internationally, there is a worldwide network of colleagues who will help redefine what international psychology can be.

Conclusion

Studying psychology in the United States as an international student can be a very rewarding experience, on both a personal and professional level. By becoming aware of the concerns covered in this chapter, you can minimize the adaptation time and get the most out of your experience.

References

Das, A. K., Chow, S. Y., & Rutherford, B. (1986). The counseling needs of foreign students. *International Journal for the Advancement of Counseling, 9,* 167–174.

Educational Testing Service. (2007a). *GRE—Graduate Record Examinations.* Retrieved June 30, 2007, from http://www.gre.org

Educational Testing Service. (2007b). *The TOEFL Test—Test of English as a Foreign Language.* Retrieved June 30, 2007, from http://www.toefl.org

Kashima, E. S., & Bundoora, V. (2006). International students' acculturation: Effects of international, conational and local ties and need for closure. *International Journal of Intercultural Relations, 30,* 471–485.

Mupinga, E. E., & Mupinga, D. M. (2005). Perceptions of international students toward GRE. *College Student Journal, 39,* 402–408.

Sam, D. L. (2001). Satisfaction with life among international students: An exploratory study. *Social Indicators Research, 53,* 315–337.

Arpana G. Inman, Jae Yeon Jeong, and Yoko Mori

Benefits and Challenges of Studying Psychology in the United States

3

P sychology is not only a popular area of study but also a well developed field in the United States. As you make decisions regarding your education and as you choose which programs or schools to attend, you should be aware of common issues that many international students face. In this chapter we highlight the specific benefits and challenges you might encounter in studying psychology in the United States, and we include several suggestions and recommendations for faculty and supervisors working with international students.

Benefits

Psychology is the study of the mind, brain, and behavior and involves the application of this knowledge to various aspects of the human experience. However, the field of psychology is quite broad and encompasses many areas of specialization. You can earn master's and doctoral degrees in clinical, consulting, counseling, developmental, educational, experimental, health, industrial/organizational, school, social, and personality psychology, to name a few areas. A detailed discussion of the subfields within psychology is beyond the scope of this chapter, but more information about the way in which some subfields are represented within the American Psychological Association (APA) is available on the APA Web site at http://www.apa.org/about/division.html. Regardless of the type of degree or area of study you choose to pursue, studying psychology in the United States has several overarching benefits. You may experience benefits in the following five areas: educational system, leadership opportunities, clinical experiences, finances, and language, each of which is discussed in the following sections.

EDUCATIONAL SYSTEM

Accreditation plays a significant role in the educational system in the United States. An accreditation process ensures standards of university training so that institutions maintain the rigor and breadth of training needed to ensure greater success and diverse opportunities in a competitive world. Six regional accrediting organizations (Middle States, New England, North Central, Northwest, Southern, and Western) set standards of education for *all* degrees at universities in a particular region. In addition to university accreditation, there are organizations that accredit academic degrees in specific subject areas (e.g., psychology, computer science). For example, in the field of psychology, practitioner-focused programs tend to be accredited over programs that prepare only researchers and scientists. Specifically, the APA is one of the major organizations that accredits psychology programs that prepare students to be clinicians and practitioners (e.g., clinical, counseling, school psychology). This accreditation serves as a quality control mechanism and allows for a uniform educational standard to be maintained within programs at different universities.

The educational system in the United States espouses values of personal responsibility, critical reflection over rote memorization, independent thinking and decision making, assertion of ideas, interactive learning, leadership skills, and diversity. To foster these values, education is approached through a blend of didactic and experiential formats. You will have excellent opportunities to develop these values and skills through educational approaches that include lectures, discussions, observations, practical application, experiential learning, and computer-based instruction (Smithee, Greenblatt, & Eland, 2004).

LEADERSHIP OPPORTUNITIES

As an international student, you can gain leadership skills that will serve you well, both in the United States and home in your country. In academic environments, you can function as a teaching assistant and engage in research activities. You can also attend national conferences and network with others in your chosen field (see chap. 14 for additional resources on professional development and networking). You can also take advantage of the many opportunities to assume leadership positions in different organizations. For example, students have been elected or appointed as committee or subcommittee chairs, committee members, and student liaisons to executive councils or other governance boards within various organizations (e.g., the American Psychological Association of Graduate Students, the Asian American Psychological Association, or Divisions within the APA). These experiences can help you to see and understand issues from different perspectives. Such perspectives can increase your confidence and your ability to critically analyze a situation from multiple perspectives.

CLINICAL EXPERIENCES

Clinical training is a primary benefit for students enrolled in applied areas of psychology (e.g., clinical, school, and counseling psychology). If you are an international student in a practitioner training program who is preparing to deliver services such as therapy, testing, assessment, or consultation, you can gain actual experience practicing your new and emerging skills through supervised clinical practica (also termed externships, fieldwork, clinical placements, and internships) in different settings (e.g., schools, community mental health agencies, or hospitals). These supervised, hands-on experiences help with the application of theoretical knowledge to practice, may last over at least two academic semesters for approximately 20 hours per week, and are typically unpaid as they are considered part of one's education. Although clinical training, rather than employment, is the primary purpose of these experiences, practica and internships may provide employment opportunities for you as an international student.

Specifically, although international students are not permitted to be employed off campus without authorization, in some instances (e.g., financial hardships) an international student may be paid while engaged in practicum training. Curricular Practical Training is one such opportunity (U.S. Immigration and Customs Enforcement, n.d.). For example, when practicum training is a required part of a training program, students on F-1 status (i.e., nonimmigrant visa status for students who are pursuing full-time studies in the United States) may be paid for their clinical work. Other paid opportunities that students can pursue include Optional Practical Training for students with F-1 status and Academic Training for students with J-1 status (i.e., nonimmigrant visa status for visiting or exchange students who intend to return to their home countries after study). Both types of training essentially supplement the academic program and may be completed before or after graduation. Because of the complexity of requirements for these paid training positions, a consultation with the International Student Service (ISS) office is strongly recommended.

FINANCES

Obtaining a degree in the United States can lead to significant financial benefits. With a degree in psychology from a U.S. university, you can expect to gain a multifaceted set of marketable skills that can serve you well in your home country or in the United States. If you stay in the United States, your job opportunities may range from being a therapist in clinics, hospitals, or university counseling centers, to acting as a consultant for businesses, faculty, or professors at universities, or working as a researcher in private companies or at universities. Additionally, obtaining a degree in the United States and returning to your home country may open doors to opportunities you might not have considered. For example, an Asian Indian international student shared that having a U.S.-based degree elevated her financial and social status as a therapist in India. For additional information on returning home, please refer to chapter 15.

LANGUAGE

If you are like many international students, you may begin your studies in the United States with a good command of the English language (e.g., having passed the standard TOEFL and other admission tests), and find that your academic training itself will further improve your language proficiency. You will find that attaining fluency in two languages is an asset within the constantly changing demographic landscape of the United States. For example, one East Asian international student reported that being bilingual allowed her to become more sensitive to the subtle cultural differences that are expressed in different languages.

Challenges

The cultural norms of your home country may be different from those in the United States, even if they are very subtle differences. Thus, developing an awareness of cultural norms and standards of behavior that may be different from your own experience is an important step in your multicultural training as an international student. If you have questions or uncertainties about certain cultural differences, there are often multiple sources of help. For example, most professors are eager to help and are excellent resources (see chap. 10 on how to work with faculty and supervisors), and the ISS office at your university can be an additional source of support (refer to chap. 4 for information on locating resources at your university; see also Smithee et al., 2004). You may find the following areas particularly challenging: cultural adjustment and shock, language, discrimination, the educational system, clinical settings, and research.

CULTURAL ADJUSTMENT AND SHOCK

As a student studying outside your home country, you may experience cultural adjustment difficulties because of a loss of support systems and a lack of knowledge about local social norms and communication patterns. One major challenge within the context of cultural adjustment is the phenomenon of *culture shock* (Chapdelaine & Alexitch, 2004). Culture shock is commonly recognized as a stress reaction resulting from an inability to understand or predict the behaviors of others when transitioning to a new cultural context. Intra- and interpersonal difficulties that arise within this context can affect the quality of your educational experience and the quality of the relationships you form in your new environment.

Being cognizant of cultural variations in interpersonal areas such as communication styles, assertiveness, personal distance, and formality in relationships will be one of the first steps you need to take to form successful relationships with peers and professors. For instance, in the United States direct communication with an assertive style such as maintaining eye contact is not only valued but also suggests that you are self-confident. If you avoid direct communication, you may be perceived as anxious, shy, or unassertive. This may lead to limited social opportunities and isolation. Depending on the geographic location of the university you attend, there may also be regional differences in the accents, slang, and jargon used in the classroom, which may take additional time for you to understand.

The level of formality and self-disclosure may also vary depending on the type of function and the relationships you form with different individuals. For instance, some faculty may expect students to address them by their first name, whereas others prefer to be called *Doctor* or *Professor* and view it as disrespectful not to be called by their formal title. Additionally, although you might expect personal issues to remain private, family or other emergencies that affect academic performance or attendance may need to be shared with faculty members (Smithee et al., 2004). In fact, some practitioner-oriented programs adhere to the idea that personal disclosure through engaging in personal therapy or reflecting on personal issues in the classroom is an important part of training to become a therapist. You are encouraged to discuss these preferences with your faculty. Adjusting to a new culture and its norms may seem overwhelming to you at times, especially when supportive personal relationships and other familiar resources may be lacking. As an international student, you may find that personal counseling and mentoring relationships are especially helpful in adjusting to and understanding your new cultural environment.

LANGUAGE

Language proficiency has been consistently linked to the academic and social adjustment of international students (Arthur, 2004). English as a Second Language programs, often available at universities, can help you assess your language proficiency and receive professional tutoring in all areas of English. Writing centers on campus can also assist you with improving your writing style and skills. As with any language, you will find that interacting with English speakers is key to improving your grasp of the spoken language. You may want to find conversational partners, attend religious services or other community group meetings, participate in study groups, sign up for English classes, or watch television shows and movies to improve your facility with the spoken language. You may also find it helpful to form a support group with fellow students struggling with their English-speaking aptitude.

DISCRIMINATION

You should be aware that you may be faced with various forms and degrees of prejudice and discrimination in your new environment. For example, international students of color may be expected or thought to represent all people from their country, regardless of regional and racial differences within their country. Some individuals you meet may believe that all people from a particular country are the same and share the exact same culture. Additionally, some educational programs in the United States tend to focus on domestic issues, so international students may believe that it is solely their responsibility to introduce global issues in class (Mittal & Wieling, 2006). Similarly, constantly being viewed as a foreigner and not "achieving an insider status" among people different from them might be another challenge (Mittal & Wieling, 2006, p. 370).

However, it is important to note that assimilating into the dominant culture is not necessarily desirable for international students. The push to assimilate by Americanizing names and taking on other Western values (e.g., speaking up in class) might be additional ways that international students experience discrimination. Alternatively, the negative and discriminatory experiences of international students from European backgrounds may be less noticeable because of racial similarities with the majority group of Americans. For instance, in some regions of the United States, people with light-colored skin who do not have obvious or lesser known accents may be perceived as American even though they are not.

Ways you can deal with any prejudice or discrimination you encounter include learning to stand up for your country and your unique experiences, showing that you are comfortable with the cultural differences between countries, letting others see that you are self-confident (Mittal & Wieling, 2006), and encouraging a broader conceptualization of diversity in the conversations and dialogues that you have with others.

THE EDUCATIONAL SYSTEM

Admission tests (which are normed on the host culture) and admission processes that are unique to each school create additional challenges for you as an international student (Smithee et al., 2004). An additional concern for you may also include struggling to understand some of your professors' examples or language patterns. Because different cultures use different pause times in spoken dialogue, you may have difficulty responding before the subject of the discussion changes (Smithee et al., 2004). For example, international students have frequently indicated that they feel at a disadvantage because people in the United States tend to speak quickly and do not leave a reasonable amount of pause time or space for them to share their thoughts. Despite many varied teaching approaches that include highly structured, lecturing, interactive, and open discussion methods (see chap. 10 for more information on teaching), teaching and learning styles that you encounter at your university in the United States may be quite different from those used in your home country. Because you may not be accustomed to these approaches, you may have to attend to details and issues that are not automatic and are not as familiar to you as they are for students from the United States, which may create more stress (Arthur, 2004). Furthermore, because of differences in cultural norms, the education you receive in the United States may not be fully applicable in your native country (see chap. 15 on returning home). However, you can deal with these difficulties by taking charge of and assuming responsibility for your educational experience. Becoming informed about your program's expectations, requirements, and deadlines and communicating with your program's faculty about pedagogical tools used in the classroom will help you get much more out of your education than if you passively try to get by.

CLINICAL SETTINGS

Clinical training is an integral part of graduate school preparation for students in school, clinical, and counseling psychology programs. The practicum is structured as a field service experience in which trainees gain awareness, knowledge, and skills in a variety of clinical tasks. In this context, guidance is provided by an experienced clinician who oversees the trainee's clinical work.

Although being a therapist is a very enriching experience, practicum experiences may bring several challenges. Despite proficiency in the English language, some students struggle with the use of slang (Chung, 1993) or a different or unusual dialect. As a result of their appearance or language differences and accents, some trainees may have the experience of clients terminating early or may have difficulty getting clients into treatment (Chung, 1993). You may find that as an international trainee, your approach to counseling and level of adjustment to the culture in the United States may affect your understanding of client issues (Chung, 1993), and in turn your sense of counseling self-efficacy (Nilsson & Anderson, 2004). For example, an international student who comes from a culture that values privacy about personal issues might struggle with asking personal questions in therapy, because in his or her culture that may be seen as being too intrusive. Maintaining an open dialogue with your supervisors and peers about cultural differences and communication styles can help you clarify any confusion, decrease anxiety, and deepen your understanding of culture in the United States.

A second potential challenge might occur at a practicum site and within the supervisory relationship. Level of readiness to accept international students at practicum sites can play a significant role not only in locating an appropriate site for a student but also for supervisors in providing effective supervision. For instance, some supervisors may not want to work with you as an international student because they believe that they may not understand you, or that it may take too much time and commitment to overcome language barriers. Such attitudes can affect supervisors' ability to work with international trainees. Similarly, because of the limited support they receive in the United States, international students tend to rely professionally and personally on relationships they develop while pursuing their training. If supervisors or faculty are not receptive to your needs, you may find that you experience social isolation and frustration within the context of your training. Contacting the training site and exploring how the training needs of other international students were addressed is one way to prepare yourself for your training experience.

Another approach in dealing with these issues is for you to recognize that one person may not be able to meet all of your needs. As an international student, you are encouraged to seek support from multiple people, services, and locations. If you depend on one particular supervisor or professor, you might be disappointed in his or her advice or the amount of time he or she has available for you; thus, seeking out only one person to rely on may not be the best approach for any international student. For more on working with faculty and supervisors, see chapter 9.

RESEARCH

As part of your training and study, you may want to conduct research related to your own culture; however, you may encounter some difficulty locating a faculty member with the requisite knowledge, experience, or interest in that particular culture. In addition, because of limited research on international issues, few scales are available that are normed on these communities. This can create further challenges in conducting research on international experiences. Some ways to address this may be for you to connect with faculty in departments or schools other than your own who may be engaged in such research. Seeking guidance from these different sources can help you develop your line of research while also offering alternate networking opportunities. In addressing the limited research on international issues, it may be helpful for you to select a qualitative research methodology that allows you to obtain in-depth information on various phenomena within a target culture (e.g., international students' experiences in supervision). However, it is important to note that some programs may discourage you from undertaking qualitative research, either because of philosophical reasons or the concern that it is too time consuming. You are encouraged to explore these issues and share your personal experiences with faculty to help increase faculty awareness about these issues (also refer to chap. 11 for information on conducting cross-cultural or international research with faculty).

Recommendations for Faculty and Supervisors Working With International Students

The literature suggests that greater support from training programs has been shown to reduce international students' stress levels. Specifically, positive relationships with faculty (Mittal & Wieling, 2006), support groups (Smith, Chin, Inman, & Findling, 1999), the availability of tangible supports (e.g., resources), and a culturally sensitive learning environment (Falender & Shafranske, 2005) have been identified as important to students' emotional, academic, and social adjustment to culture in the United States.

Faculty members ideally should acknowledge and be sensitive to international students' experiences. They can reach out to international students by inquiring about their adjustment process and teaching them about the academic culture in the United States. International students should also be encouraged to be themselves, or authentic and true to their individual cultures. Faculty can support these students in their efforts to maintain and embrace their ethnic and cultural backgrounds and avoid placing students in uncomfortable or compromising situations (e.g., asking whether they have a nickname that might be easier to pronounce). Faculty should also take steps to bring out the best in their international students by using alternative methods of assessments, providing mentoring, giving their students unique opportunities, and helping to connect students to resources and people in the university and clinical communities. Faculty should also be proactive in creating a positive learning environment by developing a broader curriculum that is inclusive of global issues, building a supportive community that validates students' experiences and prevents isolation, and sponsoring a new student orientation specific to international students' needs.

Prejudicial attitudes and discriminatory experiences can prevent international students from seeking help. Faculty can assess the internal climate of the program and collaborate with international students to create a culturally inclusive training environment in which international students are able to excel.

References

Arthur, N. (2004). *Counseling international students: Clients from around the world.* New York: Kluwer Academic/Plenum Publishers.

Chapdelaine, R. F., & Alexitch, L. R. (2004). Social skills difficulty: Model of culture shock for international graduate students. *Journal of College Student Development, 45*(2), 167–184.

Chung, Y. B. (1993). The education of international counseling psychology students in the United States. *Asian Journal of Counseling, 11*, 55–59.

Falender, C. A., & Shafranske, E. P. (2005). *Clinical supervision: A competency-based approach.* Washington, DC: American Psychological Association.

Mittal, M., & Wieling, E. (2006). Training experiences of international doctoral students in marriage and family therapy. *Journal of Marital and Family Therapy, 32*, 369–383.

Nilsson, J. E., & Anderson, M. Z. (2004). Supervising international students: The role of acculturation, role ambiguity, and multicultural discussions. *Professional Psychology: Research and Practice, 35*(3), 306–312.

Smith, T. B., Chin, L. C., Inman, A. G., & Findling, J. (1999). An outreach support group for international students. *Journal of College Counseling, 2*, 188–190.

Smithee, M., Greenblatt, S. L., & Eland, A. (2004). *U.S. culture series: U.S. classroom culture*. Washington, DC: Association of International Educators.

United States Immigration and Customs Enforcement. (n.d.). *International students: Curricular practical training*. Retrieved January 1, 2007, from http://www.ice.gov/sevis/students/cpt.htm

FUNDING RESOURCES AND LEGAL REQUIREMENTS

Suzana G. V. H. Adams, Danny Wedding, and Louise Baca

Locating International Student Resources at Your University

4

nternational students choose to study in the United States for many different reasons. Some students want to obtain an advanced degree and practical experience and with that knowledge and experience, eventually return home to pursue a career in their own countries. Others may view the move as more permanent, as they plan to live and work in the United States with their newly earned credentials. Finally, there are those who hope an international educational experience will be a way to escape their past and shape a new future by moving to a different country. Each student will have purposes, intentions, and levels of commitment that are unique; however, all international students have shared needs and expectations that must be addressed for them to stay motivated, participate fully in their educational experiences, and achieve their academic and professional goals. Thus, locating resources is essential for academic success.

Questions You May Want to Ask When Selecting a University

Before you choose the university you will be attending, it is important to ask some hard questions. Although some questions may seem abstract and you might initially feel uncomfortable asking them, doing so will dramatically enhance the likelihood that you will pick a university that has the academic, intellectual, and infrastructural resources necessary to support education for an international student. You may want to create a table populated with the answers you receive to your questions to compare and contrast one university with another and establish the minimum criteria for your choice.

We recommend that you ask yourself the following questions about every school you are considering attending: Does the university truly value multicultural perspectives? If so, how do the philosophy and values of the institution relate to international students? How does the university participate in cultural events relevant to the local community (e.g., celebration of *Dia de los Muertos*)? Does the university foster intercultural understanding? Do faculty members publish in international journals? Has the faculty participated in relevant international educational programs, such as the Fulbright Fellowship Program? How many members of the faculty are fluent in more than one language, and which languages do they speak? Do faculty members of the psychology department belong to relevant divisions of the American Psychological Association (APA) or similar organizations (e.g., Division 52 [International Psychology] of APA or the International Society of Clinical Psychology)? Do faculty members participate and present papers at international conferences, such as the quadrennial International Congresses of Psychology or the quadrennial meetings of the International Association of Applied Psychology? Do current international students feel that the faculty genuinely values differences in nationality, race, culture, age, socioeconomic level, and language? Are these values reflected in the curriculum and classroom activities? How is the university's nondiscrimination policy applied if a student believes that he or she has been discriminated against or harassed on the basis of race, color, nationality, sex, gender, sexual orientation, disability, age, or religion? If you are applying to clinical or counseling psychology programs, how do those candidate universities support culturally responsive therapy and supervision?[1]

You should ask all these questions—and many others—before choosing a university. You have every right to ask these questions and to receive clear, sufficiently detailed answers. Unfortunately, these questions

---

[1]Culturally responsive therapy and supervision represents new territory for many professors in higher education. Having wonderful students bring all of their rich heritage to the process of psychotherapy means making changes in our expectations for evaluations such as comprehensive exams. Because of a courageous Latina student who wanted to provide culturally and linguistically appropriate services to her Spanish-speaking clients, Argosy University changed its requirements to accommodate this student and better meet the needs of the people she serves. Following her lead, three other Latino students submitted evaluation samples of their work in Spanish. Now, instead of this process becoming an exception to the rule, it has resulted in a change of policy that allows students to submit their work samples in a language other than English. This is a marvelous first step toward cultural competency. (L. B.)

are not asked often enough, sometimes out of fear that the answers obtained may rule out a particular university as a viable educational option. It should be noted that answers to these questions are also important for international students transitioning into the professional world. We especially recommend that you seek out and interview other international students who are finishing the program in which you are interested and already "know the road ahead."

APPROACHES TO LOCATING INTERNATIONAL RESOURCES AFTER YOU ARE ACCEPTED

International students sometimes find it difficult to locate all the relevant social, academic, financial, and legal resources available at their university, yet there are almost always abundant resources. You should keep in mind that the quality of the international experience will be diminished if you fail to seek out and exploit the learning opportunities associated with these resources.

The ability to identify and take advantage of relevant resources is tightly linked with the process of acculturation. For example, some international students never achieve any degree of acculturation and they remain isolated or spend most of their time with other international students or sometimes only with other students from their home country. Of course, mastering the process of acculturating means to be willing to be open to the opportunities offered by the dominant culture, while at the same time honoring the defining aspects of one's native culture. If you make a deliberate decision to become involved with as many different cultures as possible—and especially with the culture of your host country—you are far more likely to come to appreciate the varied culture of the United States and benefit much more from your international study experience.

You may sometimes find it difficult to remain engaged with the world you left behind, while at the same time you are trying to be open to the new experiences that international education makes possible. Finding yourself in between cultures requires tremendous flexibility. In this process it is helpful to belong to an association in which other students and professors share information and give support to each other, thus functioning something like a second family. Associations can already be part of a university system (e.g., University of Illinois, see http://www.ips.uiuc.edu/isss) or can be part of a larger network, such as the National Latina/o Psychological Association (NLPA; see http://www.nlpa.ws). Another option you may want to explore is to create your own association with like-minded students; examples, as well as assistance, can be found through your university's representatives or through organizations such as National Association of Foreign Student Advisers (NAFSA; see http://www.nafsa.org).[2]

In addition, you will be asked to meet the same academic requirements as every other student, native or not, and because you may not be fully conversant with English or may not have taken many psychology courses, you may lack experience with something as simple as putting references in APA style, making footnotes, or formatting a research paper. There are usually formal organizations designed to help with these problems. Almost every American university has a writing lab or writing assistants who welcome the opportunity to assist international students. However, opportunities such as these are only available to those students who are resourceful enough to identify the opportunities and pursue them aggressively.

Universities vary in their commitment to international education, and in any given setting there may be considerable differences across programs and participating faculty in their interest in international education and their enthusiasm for working with international students. However, most universities have professors who are genuinely interested in international issues and who deliberately seek out international students and the opportunity to work with them. It is especially helpful when senior academic administrators value international students, actively work to engage these students in campus life, make time to host events, and look for opportunities to recognize and congratulate those faculty members who have reached out to support and mentor international students.

Locating the campus resources that you need often requires understanding university politics and how your university's international office works (or fails to work). To obtain and organize resources and support, you need to build and maintain interpersonal relationships with all members of your university community, including advisors, research professors, committee members, and fellow students.

You can find resources relating to international students in both international student centers and international student offices located on large university campuses. If the university is small, you may find resources for international students in departments called *student services, student affairs,* or *office of student life;* some universities have a dean of student life who manages a team of people and functions responsible for

---

[2]One Student's Experience of Building an Intracultural Bridge: During the various phases of development in my four years as an international student, I realized that in order for me to communicate more effectively with the university, I had to maintain a balance between the greater worldview and the more specific one of the university. To do that, I joined both APA Division 52 (International Psychology) and the NLPA and found advisors who were able to mentor me. They provided an intracultural bridge that has helped me challenge old ethical biases and negotiate the application of current APA multicultural guidelines. (S. A.)

organized student activities, support to students, and who sometimes acts as an ombudsman representing students before the university. The people who work in these areas are usually trained to assist students in finding the help they need, even if they do not have exactly the information requested during the initial contact. Finally, if none of these resources are available to you, you may want to be a pioneer and create these resources. You are part of an ethnic, linguistic, and culturally diverse population as well as a larger system that you can enrich by sharing your experience. Communicating your needs is necessary to reach cultural mutuality.

HOW TO COMMUNICATE YOUR NEEDS TO THE UNIVERSITY

It is important to learn to be patient with individuals who have trouble understanding English when it is spoken with any type of accent (or worse, with those individuals who stop trying to understand what a student is saying after they realize they are speaking with an international student). It is critical that you communicate your tangible and perceived needs, as well as the cultural values that are attached to them, because assumptions and misinterpretations can often lead to conflict. As a result, you may not feel "listened to" and you may sense from others a lack of trust and respect. Understand that the expectations of both international students and faculty members are culturally tinted. You may see your alma mater (university) as your surrogate family and may expect consistent support and fluid communication. However, verbal and nonverbal communication is often ambiguous in the academic family; assertive communication needs to be practiced with varying degrees of directness.

Many international students are more fluent in written than in spoken English; however, some people may not be sensitive to this distinction. If you tell a representative from the university what your primary language is, the representative may be able to identify another individual within the university community who speaks your language and who might become a friend, a support, or even a mentor. To ensure that communication is clear, you can also ask for this type of help as you begin to communicate with people on campus. You should not hesitate to ask for repetition or clarification if you do not understand clearly what is being said, and you should follow up your conversations with a written letter or e-mail. This will minimize the likelihood of confusion and misunderstanding. It is useful to keep copies of all relevant e-mail communication and to have all this information with you when you visit a university campus.

WHAT YOU SHOULD DO IF YOUR UNIVERSITY DOES NOT ANSWER YOUR QUESTIONS

You need to recognize that you will not always have all your questions answered. However, numerous resources are available to you in addition to those already discussed in this chapter. Many of these are available on the Internet or as documents available from the U.S. federal government. For example, educationUSA (see http://www.educationusa.state.gov), NAFSA: Association of International Educators (see http://www.nafsa.org), and International Student and Study Abroad Resource Center (see http://www.internationalstudent.com) can help you if you are a student who is just beginning to search for an international opportunity in the United States. These organizations address many of the core issues associated with international education (e.g., getting a visa, obtaining financial assistance, and the relative costs of public and private institutions). However, we continue to believe that other international students—even if they are not from your country—are the best source of information about how to cope with the challenges and how to maximize the professional and personal growth potential associated with international education. Union gives strength.

Priscilla Dass-Brailsford and Benjamin Siankam

Funding Opportunities for International Students

5

S tudents in the United States have the opportunity to study at a large selection of good quality colleges and universities, and this range of educational programs makes American schools attractive to prospective international students. In fact, the American Psychological Association (APA) identifies over 500 graduate programs in psychology at American universities. However, increasing higher education costs and the complex application process can discourage some international students from applying. If you want to study in the United States, you must weigh the costs and benefits of pursuing advanced study and must use careful financial planning early in the application process.

Data from the 2002 through 2003 academic year indicated that U.S. colleges and universities offered financial support to 38% of their international graduate students and 9% of their international undergraduate students (College Board, 2004), suggesting that graduate students are more likely than undergraduate students to receive funding. However, a report from the July–August 2006 issue of the *APA Monitor on Psychology* analyzed trends for new psychology graduates and found that although 70% of doctoral students received some university-based support, 86% used their own or family resources to pay for graduate education. About 60% obtained student loans to complete their education (Bailey, 2006). The report also showed that graduate students matriculating in doctoral programs in clinical psychology (PsyD and PhD) were likely to incur up to four times more debt (average debt from $50,000 to $90,000) than those students who pursued research subfields (average debt of $21,500) with ready access to research funding opportunities.

The majority of international students in the United States depend on either personal or family support for educational funding. The *International Student Handbook for Undergraduate and Graduate Students* reported that in the academic year 2003 through 2004, approximately 51% of international students personally financed their education (College Board, 2004), and the *Hobsons U.S. Education Guide* reported an even higher percentage of about two thirds (Marchesani, 2006). These reports are corroborated by that of the Organization for Economic Co-operation and Development, which showed that 66% of international students in the United States were supported by personal or family resources.

In this chapter, we discuss the challenges you face in financing your education in the United States. We then discuss potential sources of funding and financial aid opportunities that can assist you in the decision-making process.

Tuition and Fees

The expenses involved in studying in the United States range from tuition fees to housing, transportation, and other living expenses. If you are a prospective student whose native language is not English, there may be the extra cost of taking English language classes. In addition, health insurance is a mandated requirement for all students studying in the United States, which is an added financial expense for you.

All international students who apply for admission to a U.S. university are required to submit a certification of finances, which outlines a student's financial resources. Admission to an institution of higher education ultimately depends on your ability to demonstrate sufficient financial support to cover the total projected costs of your education. The prospective educational institution, following strict government regulations, is required to verify the financial resources of all international student applicants before the I-20 or DS-2019 Certificate of Eligibility forms are issued. This certificate is required when you apply for the F-1 (student) or J-1 (exchange visitor) visa, which will allow you entrance into the United States.

You are encouraged to inquire whether prospective schools provide grants, loans, or scholarships for international students. This will ultimately determine whether you have to fund your education yourself or change your school to one that can offer funding. Some universities offer financial aid awards to a small group of entering international students through scholarships, grants, and graduate assistantships. These awards are need-based, limited, and competition to secure them is fierce. Schools are usually careful to help the most deserving international students.

Specific, selective admission criteria (good grades, high scores on the Scholastic Aptitude Test or the Graduate Record Examination, and strong letters of recommendation), as well as the amount of financial aid requested by an applicant, are major factors that influence an admission committee's decision. As a result, candidates who may be well qualified but who are without adequate financial resources may not be offered admission. Thus, the admission rate for international applicants requesting financial aid is substantially lower than for those not requesting aid (Pate, 2001).

Tuition is a major expense for any graduate education. *Graduate Study in Psychology*, a publication of the APA, provides valuable and up-to-date information on almost 600 graduate programs in psychology in the United States and Canada. In addition to admission requirements and deadlines, the publication includes information about tuition, the amount of potential financial support, and the percentage of students who received financial support in past years.

The cost of tuition can vary widely among institutions of higher learning. Tuition at private institutions can be five times higher than tuition at public and state institutions (Pate, 2001). International students do not qualify for the benefits of reduced in-state resident tuition because this is only available to United States citizens who are permanent residents of the state in which the university they are applying to is located. Tuition at private institutions tends to be steep, sometimes costing twice as much as the tuition a nonresident student at a public state university pays (Pate, 2001). Thus, even without the benefits of being the resident of a particular state, enrolling at a state institution may remain the most cost-effective option for an international student. This should be weighed against the fact that although private colleges tend to be more expensive, they sometimes offer larger stipends than public institutions (Pate, 2001). In addition, they require students who receive funding to work about 16 hours per week, compared with public universities, which require about 20 hours of work per week. Finally, doctoral students in psychology who attend public universities can expect to pay almost twice as much in total tuition as their counterparts in terminal master's degree programs, in large part because of the longer period it takes to complete a doctoral program (Pate, 2001).

HOUSING AND LIVING EXPENSES

Besides tuition, as a prospective student you have to consider the overall costs of room and board, transportation, and other living expenses before accepting an offer from an educational institution. For most international students, housing will be the second largest expense, after tuition. Although some graduate programs offer on-campus accommodations, most do not. Chances are good that you will need to find off-campus housing. Housing costs may vary significantly on the basis of the location of the school; regional living expenses also differ greatly. Urban areas are likely to be more expensive than rural ones, and housing expenses in the South and Midwest regions of the United States are lower than on the East and West coasts.

The Internet can be an invaluable research tool for you as you seek housing, as it can be used to compare housing and cost of living expenses in the different regions of the United States. One of the most popular Web sites identified in the *Hobsons U.S. Education Guide 2006,* http://www.bestplaces.net, used the Bureau of Labor Statistics Consumer Price Index to provide information on cost of living expenses in the United States. For example, cost of living indicators from the Web site suggest that graduate students studying in New York City can expect to spend 35% more for off-campus housing than their counterparts in St. Louis, Missouri. Sharing accommodations with roommates is an efficient way to reduce rental costs and utility bills.

Expenses for food, transportation, and utilities also vary from one region to another. Compared with the national average, combined expenses for food, transportation, and utilities are over 40% higher in New York City, 10% higher in Honolulu, Hawaii, and 3% lower in St. Louis, Missouri (http://www.bestplaces.net). Big cities and urban areas tend to have better and more reliable public transportation systems. As a result, students in New York City can expect to complete their entire graduate education without incurring motor vehicle expenses. In contrast, students who attend colleges and universities in outlying areas may benefit from lower living expenses but may have the additional cost of purchasing, maintaining, and insuring a vehicle.

WORKING IN THE UNITED STATES

Your employment opportunities while on a student visa in the United States are limited, and the rules of employment are strictly enforced. Even if you plan to work while studying you are unlikely to earn enough to cover the costs of all your expenses, which include room and board, transportation, living expenses, and possibly English language classes.

On-Campus Employment

Students on an F-1 visa (student visa) or a J-1 visa (exchange visitor visa) are eligible only to work part time, for 20 hours per week while school is in session (they can work more hours during the summer and during vacation periods). As an international student, you are not eligible for jobs funded by the federal work–study program. On-campus employment includes teaching–research assistantships, jobs in dining services, libraries, and other campus offices. Student jobs are often advertised at the various locations frequented by students on campus. Students are only allowed to work on the campus of the school that issued the original I-20/DS-2019 form (the certificate of eligibility needed to get a student visa). This means that transfer students have to finalize the F-1 or J-1 visa transfer before the first day of employment.

Although international students may not qualify for all types of assistance (e.g., those that are federally funded), they do qualify for teaching and research assistantships, which are the most common types of funding provided to graduate students. Moreover, before applying to a preferred program, as a prospective student you can contact the director or recruiter of the program to inquire about available funding.

Off-Campus Employment

If you plan to work off campus, you must receive employment authorization prior to beginning the employment. The international student office at the university at which you are enrolled can help you obtain approval for off-campus employment. To further help with your planning, organizational resources for funding are outlined in the following sections of this chapter.

INSTITUTE OF INTERNATIONAL EDUCATION

The Institute of International Education (IIE) is an independent, nonprofit organization. It is one of the largest and most experienced American higher education exchange agencies, with over 850 college and university members in the United States and abroad. IIE publishes some useful texts that we discuss in detail.

Funding U.S. Studies: Graduate and Postgraduate Opportunities for Latin Americans

This reference book describes various financial assistance opportunities for prospective students from Latin America and the Caribbean who are interested in graduate level study and research in the United States. It provides information on funding for graduate study, doctoral and postdoctoral research opportunities, and work–study grants available through foundation and institutional scholarship programs and institutional grant opportunities, as well as information on special programs such as the Fulbright and Ford fellowships. It includes a comprehensive listing of United States educational counseling centers in Latin America where students can seek educational advising and further explore university and funding opportunities. The reference includes informative articles on academic cultural preparation for life in the United States.

Funding for U.S. Studies: A Scholarship Guide for Europeans

This guide provides students from Europe with detailed information about scholarships, grants, and fellowships for graduate study. The guide also contains information on doctoral and postdoctoral research opportunities in the United States that are available through U.S. and foreign governments, colleges and universities, educational associations, libraries, research centers, foundations, corporations, and other organizations. Each description includes contact information, purpose of the award, amount and type of award, location of study, eligibility requirements, restrictions and duration, application deadlines, notification dates, and application details. In addition, the guide has informative articles on financial assistance and university funding options, as well as a comprehensive listing of United States educational counseling centers in Europe where students can research university and funding opportunities.

Funding for U.S. Studies: A Guide for International Students, Scholars, and Professionals

This guide lists over 500 available grants and scholarships, and is a valuable resource for both advisors and the international students they counsel. It provides detailed descriptions of grants, fellowships, and scholarships that are available for undergraduate and graduate study, and it also provides information on doctoral and postdoctoral research opportunities in the United States. The guide includes the grants, fellowships, and scholarships that are available through U.S. and foreign governments, colleges and universities, educational associations, research centers, libraries, foundations, corporations, and other organizations. In addition, this guide provides informative articles on financial assistance and university funding options.

FULBRIGHT SCHOLARSHIP PROGRAM

In 1945, Senator J. William Fulbright introduced a bill in the United States Congress to fund the international exchange of students in the fields of education, culture, and science. One year later, President Harry S. Truman signed the bill into law. The Fulbright Program, which is overseen by a 12-member board appointed by the president of the United States, has since become the largest U.S. international exchange program with the primary goal of increasing mutual understanding between the people of the United States and other countries.

The Fulbright Scholarship Program receives funding from an annual appropriation by the U.S. Congress to the Department of State. Participating governments and host institutions in foreign countries as well as in the United States, contribute financially to the program through cost sharing and indirect support (e.g., salary supplements, tuition waivers, and university housing). Since its establishment, more than 147,000 international students have visited the United States on Fulbright scholarships.

ADDITIONAL ORGANIZATIONS

You can also look for scholarships, student loans, and other forms of financial aid through international humanitarian organizations that promote international education and cultural exchange with the United States. These organizations include the United Nations, the World Health Organization, the League of Red Cross Societies, and the World Council of Churches. However, some of these organizations have guidelines and restrictions about eligibility for their financial aid awards. For example, international student scholarships may only be available to graduate students from a specific ethnic group or for a specific course of study. Obtaining financial aid and scholarships from humanitarian organizations is very competitive, and prospective students are wise to initiate this process early.

Finally, if you need financial aid or an international student scholarship to fund an American education, you are encouraged to seek support from within your home country. There may be international student scholarships, international student loans, or government grants available to support study abroad. Usually, a branch or sector of your home government (e.g., the ministry of higher education, embassy, or consulate in the United States) can provide this information. Your government may cover the cost of tuition fees and living expenses in return for a commitment to work in your country after graduation (College Board, 2004). Local businesses, organizations, and foundations in your home country may also offer scholarships and grants that will ease the financial burden of studying in the United States.

WEB SITE RESOURCES FOR FINANCIAL AID

Technological advances have made the Internet an efficient way for international students to research sources of financial aid. You should be aware, however, that access to some Web sites may require registration or subscription. Eligibility criteria for grants vary; some grants require United States citizenship or permanent residency. Most of the Web sites, outlined in Appendix B, were identified through the IIE, the College

Board, and *Hobsons U.S. Education Guide.* Comprehensive information about funding for international students may also be obtained at university libraries. The resources cited in Appendix B are provided to assist prospective students in identifying sources of financial assistance; it does not constitute an endorsement of these sources.

Conclusion

As an international student planning to pursue graduate education in the United States, you are encouraged to begin the application process as early as possible. Your choice of university depends on a myriad of factors, and foremost among them are the availability of funding and your financial resources. If you are able to work on or off campus, you may thus have an additional source to supplement your income.

Two organizations based in the United States that are potential resources for funding are the IIE and the Fulbright Scholarship program. International humanitarian organizations such as the United Nations, the World Health Organization, and the World Council of Churches are additional sources of support. Global technological progress will give you many opportunities to search and make applications for funding over the Internet. Financial considerations, such as the affordability of tuition costs and the availability of funding, will ultimately help you decide which offer to accept and which university you will be attending.

References

American Psychological Association. (2006). *Graduate study in psychology 2007.* Washington, DC: Author.

Bailey, D. S. (2006). Trends for new graduates. *Monitor on Psychology, 37,* p. 54.

Center for Educational Research and Innovation. (2004). *Internationalization and trade in higher education: Opportunities and challenges.* Paris, France: Organization for Economic Co-operation and Development.

College Board. (2004). *International student handbook 2005.* New York: Author.

Hobsons. (2005). *The Hobsons U.S. education guide 2006.* Cincinnati, OH: Author.

Institute of International Education. (2004). *Funding U.S. studies: Graduate and postgraduate opportunities for Latin Americans.* New York: Author.

Institute of International Education. (2005). *Funding U.S. studies: A scholarship guide for Europeans.* New York: Author.

Institute of International Education. (2007). *Funding for United States studies: A guide for international students, scholars, and professionals.* New York: Author.

Marchesani, K. (2006). *Financial aid on the Web. The Hobsons U.S. education guide 2006: Worldwide edition.* Cincinnati, OH: Hobsons.

Pate, W. E., II, (2001). *Analyses of data from graduate study in psychology: 1999–2000.* Retrieved August 10, 2007, from http://research.apa.org/grad00contents.html#tuit

Taneisha S. Buchanan and Jieun Lee

Visa and Work Permits 6

I n this chapter we provide an overview of the guidelines for obtaining and maintaining lawful international student status in the United States. Additionally, we discuss considerations regarding working with student status (e.g., on-campus employment, practical training) and obtaining work permits.

Student and Exchange Visitor Visas

Citizens of other countries generally must obtain a visa to enter the United States. The visa type is based on the purpose of travel and is defined by immigration law. There are many types of visas, but we limit our discussion to visas and work permits most likely to be used by individuals studying and working in the field of psychology. There are two types of nonimmigrant student visas: the F-1 student visa and the M-1 visa. The F-1 visa is the most commonly issued visa for students engaging in academic studies in the United States. The M-1 visa is issued to students pursuing vocational and nonacademic programs. Psychology programs are considered academic programs, so we do not discuss the M-1 visa in detail in this chapter. International students may also study in the United States on an exchange visitor visa, or the J-1 visa. The J-1 visa is for individuals participating in educational or cultural exchange programs. To be eligible for a J-1 visa, applicants must first be accepted into an exchange visitor program through a sponsoring organization (e.g., a university). The organization must receive authorization from the U.S. Department of State to offer an exchange visitor program and is then referred to as a designated sponsoring organization.

APPLYING FOR A STUDENT VISA OR EXCHANGE VISITOR VISA

The first step you need to take in the application process is to obtain a Student Exchange and Visitor Information System (SEVIS)-generated document. This document is prepared by a college or university after you have been accepted there as an incoming student. For the F-1 visa, this document is the Form I-20, Certificate of Eligibility for Nonimmigrant (F-1) Student Status. For Academic and Language Students, and for the J-1 visa, this document is a DS-2019, Certificate of Eligibility for Exchange Visitor Status. In order for the school to prepare a SEVIS-generated document, you will be required to submit documentation of financial support to cover the estimated tuition and living expenses (this estimate is typically provided by the school). Financial support documentation may include scholarship and assistantship funding documents (e.g., a contract specifying the amount and duration of the assistantship), bank statements if you are funding your own education, and affidavits of support and bank statements from friends, family, or other persons providing sponsorship.

An interview at the embassy consular section is usually required, and as a student visa applicant you must provide the SEVIS-generated document, completed visa application form, a photograph (formatted for visa purposes), a passport that will be valid for at least 6 months after the proposed program start date, and a receipt showing payment of the visa application fee and the SEVIS fee. Other fees may apply, including a nonimmigrant visa application processing fee (consult the U.S. Citizenship and Immigration Services [USCIS] Web site at http://www.uscis.gov/portal/site/uscis for fee amounts). Also, you should be prepared with transcripts and diplomas, standardized test scores required by the school (e.g., GRE scores), and documents providing evidence that your finances are sufficient to cover your estimated tuition and living expenses. During the interview, you are likely to be asked to undergo a fingerprint scan (this is a required part of the visa application process).

As an international student, you should submit visa applications as soon as possible because special clearances may be required depending on your course of study or nationality. Visas will not be issued earlier than 120 days before the proposed date of entry; however, applying before this time will allow the consulate or embassy to process any additional clearances ahead of time. The Department of Homeland Security regulations do not permit students to enter the United States earlier than 30 days before the start of their program. If you wish to do so, you must enter on a visitor visa rather than the F-1 or J-1 visa. However, this is not recommended because you will then need to apply for and receive a change of status before you begin the program of study.

Dependents

Spouses and children may also apply for visas and accompany a student to the United Status. Dependents of F-1 students will require F-2 visas and those of J-1 exchange visitors, J-2 visas. Dependents may apply for their visas along with, or after the F-1 or J-1 visa holder's application, but not before. If international students' spouses or children will be visiting for vacation only, they may be eligible to apply for a visitor visa (B-2), or if they qualify, they may travel without a visa under the Visa Waiver Program (VWP). Nationals of countries participating in the VWP do not need a visa to travel to the United States for business or tourism if the trip is to last under 90 days. The U.S. Department of State Web site (http://travel.state.gov) provides a list of countries participating in the VWP. F-2 dependents may not work or study while in the United States. J-2 dependents may study, and if they wish to be employed while in the United States, they must apply for an Employment Authorization Document from the U.S. Department of Homeland Security USCIS.

Arrival at a United States Port of Entry

On your arrival in the United States, the immigration inspector will look at the appropriate visa page in your passport and will examine supporting documents. These supporting documents include Form I-20 (F-1 students) or Form DS-2019 (J-1 students). As an international student, you should also have documents providing proof of funding in case this is requested. When you are admitted into the country, the immigration inspector will keep part of the I-94 form that you completed on the plane and will return the bottom portion to you. This portion will contain the following information: date and place of entry, a notation about the visa status through which you received entry, and the length of your stay (often indicated as *duration of status* [D/S]) at the port of entry. Although Canadian citizens do not need a visa to enter the United States, Canadians who plan to study in the United States should present their supporting documents and request F-1 or J-1 status when they arrive at the port of entry. These students will receive the I-94 form with the date of entry, status, and the period of stay.

Important Documents

In addition to your passport, which should contain a valid U.S. visa, the I-94 and I-20 or DS-2019 are two other important immigration documents that you need. The I-94 is the small card received on arrival in the United States. Although the visa indicates eligibility for admission into the country, actual admission into the United States is determined by immigration officials at the port of entry. The I-94 documents your admission status and you should keep a photocopy of both sides of the document. In most cases, you will be required to submit your I-94 at departure from the United States, even if for a short period of time; you will receive a new one on reentry. The original I-20 or DS-2019 forms should not be discarded, even if new ones are received.

Maintaining Legal Student Status in the United States

HEALTH INSURANCE AND MEDICAL TESTING

According to federal regulations, J-1 students are required to have comprehensive medical insurance that covers themselves and their dependents. F-1 students do not have the same requirement; however, most schools require all F-1 students and their dependents to enroll in the student insurance program sponsored by the university or to obtain comparable insurance coverage. As many universities include health insurance coverage in their fees, you should check to see if this benefit is provided by your chosen school. Student insurance plans may or may not cover dental or vision services, as these plans vary considerably in their coverage.

Some universities require all international students to obtain tuberculosis (TB) skin tests on arrival. Other universities only require testing for international students from countries designated by the World Health Organization as being at high risk for TB. Testing positive for TB may or may not affect a student's ability to enroll in classes (depending on the specific university's regulations), but treatment would be recommended. If testing is required for continued enrollment, this must be completed or it may affect a student's status.

EXPIRATION DATES AND AUTHORIZATION OF STAY

The I-94 determines the authorized length of stay for international students. When students arrive in the United States on a student visa, they will usually be admitted for the D/S. If students' I-94 indicates D/S for the length of their stay, they will have legal student status as long as they are a full-time student and do not violate F-1 or J-1 visa status requirements, even if their visas expire during this time. Your passport and I-20 or DS-2019, however, must not expire while you are in the United States or you will be out of status. If your passport expires, it must be renewed either through the appropriate embassy in the United States or when you return to visit your home country. If your passport expires before your U.S. visa does, you may travel with both your new passport and the expired one containing the valid visa (the visa page should not be removed). However, if you are returning home, you must have a valid visa to return to the United States (for more information about visa applications, visit the U.S. Department of State Web site at http://www.unitedstatesvisas.gov). The I-20 or DS-2019 must be valid all the time. If you need more time to complete the program of study than is indicated on the I-20 or DS-2019, you must apply for an extension before the expiration date. You should consult with your designated school official (DSO) regarding the documents (e.g., a previously issued I-20 form, a letter from your academic advisor, a transcript) that you might need to apply for an extension.

After completing the program of study listed on the Certificate of Eligibility (I-20 or DS-2019) and any authorized practical training, you are allowed additional time in the country before you must depart from the United States. You will have 60 days to prepare to leave or transfer to another school. Exchange visitors and dependents have a 30-day grace period from the program end date indicated on Form DS-2019 to leave the country. Staying beyond the authorized length of time, even by 1 day, is a violation of U.S. law and, in turn, will result in a student being considered out of status. This will require that the student apply for a new visa, typically in his or her home country.

J-1 exchange visitors must return to their home country for a 2-year foreign residency requirement after completion of their program and any authorized training if (a) they were funded by the U.S. government or government of their nationality or last residence; (b) they are nationals or residents of a country designated as a country that requires services of individuals with the specialized training that the exchange visitor was engaged in; or (c) they received graduate medical education training. J-1 visa holders meeting the conditions for the foreign residency requirement cannot change visa status before returning to their home country for a 2-year period. This requirement may be waived under the following circumstances: (a) if a U.S. citizen or permanent resident spouse or the children of the exchange visitor claims exceptional hardship if the exchange visitor is required to leave the country; (b) if the exchange visitor will be persecuted on return to the home country; (c) if a request is made on the exchange visitor's behalf by a U.S. government agency; (d) if a No Objection Statement is provided by the exchange visitor's home country; and (e) if a request is made by a designated state health department or its equivalent.

TRANSFERRING TO A DIFFERENT SCHOOL

F-1students who are currently enrolled in a school in the United States and who wish to transfer to a different school within the United States must obtain a new I-20 from the new school. To proceed with the transfer, those students need to provide their current school's DSO with the correct school code for the new school and with the name of the new school in the SEVIS system. Students will also need to work with the DSO to set their transfer release date, depending on their travel and work plans. On the transfer release dates the new schools will receive the students' records in SEVIS and the students should contact the DSO at their new schools to create a Form I-20 issued for *reason of transfer,* which will have the students' new program start dates.

TRAVELING OUTSIDE THE UNITED STATES

If you wish to travel outside the United States, you must consult your DSO at the international student office prior to your departure. Students who were registered in National Security Entry/Exit Registration Systems need to follow the appropriate exit procedure (for more information about the exit procedure, see the document at http://www.ice.gov/doclib/pi/specialregistration/WalkawayMaterial.pdf). Before you travel outside the United States, there are several important things to consider. First, you have to obtain a valid signature on your SEVIS Form I-20 or DS-2019 from your DSO if you are an F-1 visa holder, or from your responsible officer if you are a J-1 exchange visitor. Each signature is valid for a year while you are a full-time student. If you are working with the international student office, you need to bring a copy of your transcript (an unofficial transcript is sufficient) and evidence of financial information (e.g., bank statement, letter stating that you are receiving an assistantship). Second, you must check whether your visa and passport are still valid. A current passport should be valid for at least 6 months after the date of the reentry or, if you are from one of the countries that have an agreement with the United States allowing entry with a passport until the date of the expiration, you will be allowed to enter on a current passport up to the actual date of expiration.

Employment for F-1 and J-1 students

In this section we discuss two types of employment: on-campus employment and off-campus employment. In terms of on-campus employment, if you are an F-1 or J-1 student, you can work up to 20 hours per week either at the school at which you are registered or at an off-campus location that is educationally affiliated with your program or school during the school year (you must obtain permission from your international programs office). You are not allowed to work additional hours if you are already working 20 hours on campus. During school vacations, you may be employed up to 40 hours per week. Regarding off-campus employment, you need authorization from USCIS prior to your employment. Authorization will be granted for economic hardship, curricular practical training (F-1), optional practical training (F-1), academic training (J-1), and interning with an international organization. You may apply for employment based on economic need if you cannot continue your course of study because of unforeseen economic hardship or emergency circumstances. To be qualified, you have to be in good academic standing, have been registered at the school for at least one academic year, and be able to submit documentation regarding the circumstance that led to the economic hardship. You must be able to maintain full-time student status while you are employed under this provision. There are also conditions and restrictions of employment for students experiencing economic hardship, including (a) students may work off campus for up to 20 hours per week while school is in session or full time during summer or winter break, and (b) this authorization will allow students to work off campus for up to 1 year with a possible extension. Students are also permitted to work as off-campus interns at an international organization (e.g., the United Nations, the World Bank).

Two types of applied training experiences available to F-1 students are curricular practical training (CPT) and optional practical training (OPT). F-1 students may be eligible for CPT authorization for either work experience that is required for graduation, or for work experience that is not necessary for graduation but will receive academic credit. For some psychology graduate students (e.g., counseling psychology, clinical psychology) an internship is a required part of their program, and they will need to apply for CPT for their internship. When students obtain CPT authorization, they will receive a new SEVIS I-20 and will need to register for academic credit for the work they will be performing. There is no limitation in terms of the length of time students will be involved in full-time CPT. However, if students use full-time CPT for 12 months or more, they lose the option of pursuing OPT. Students who are pursuing a psychology internship should note that students who are not permanent residents or citizens of the United States are not eligible for federally funded internships (e.g., at Veterans Affairs hospitals); however, they may be eligible for internships at consortiums associated with federally funded agencies as long as they are not hired directly through these agencies.

F-1 students are eligible for 12 months of OPT per each degree that they obtain (e.g., bachelor's degree, master's degree) when moving from a lower degree program to a higher degree program (i.e., from bachelor's to master's degree or from master's degree to doctoral degree). Eligible students may apply for *precompletion OPT* (i.e., before completion of program) or *postcompletion OPT* (i.e., after completion of program). Students who apply for postcompletion OPT must check with their DSO on the minimum amount of time to apply for OPT, as the USCIS must receive their application no later than 1 week before the completion of their study and processing times vary, depending on the university. It is recommended that students apply for OPT 3 or 4 months before they wish to begin employment, because it can take up to 3 months to obtain OPT authorization. It is also recommended that students not wait too long to apply for OPT, as authorization will not extend more than 14 months after the completion of the program.

J-1 students may be eligible for academic training during their program if it is an integral part of their course of study. They may also do it on completion of their program. Typically, academic training (AT) is authorized for a maximum of 18 months, but some postdoctoral research and teaching positions may qualify for up to 36 months of academic training. The length of AT cannot be longer than the amount of time a J-1 student has been studying in their program in the United States.

H-1B: Employment-Based Visa

The H-1B visa is a nonimmigrant visa issued to persons who will be employed in a specialty occupation. A specialty occupation is one that requires at least a bachelor's degree and a specialized body of knowledge; therefore, this visa is likely to be one that most psychology graduates seeking employment in the United States would require. To apply for an H-IB visa, you must have a sponsoring U.S. employer. First, the employer will need to file a labor condition application (LCA) with the U.S. Department of Labor. The employer will then submit the certified LCA, a Form I-129 petition, and the required fee to USCIS for approval. After approval has been received, you can file for an H-1B visa, admission to the United States, or change of status if currently in the United States. Each year there is an annual limit on the number of H-1B visas issued. However, there are additional H-1B visas available if an individual has earned a master's degree or higher from a U.S. institution of higher learning (approximately 20,000 visas). If students have applied for visas for employment at an institution of higher education, a nonprofit or affiliated organization, a nonprofit research organization, or a governmental research organization, there is no limit on the number of these visas that may be issued (U.S. Citizenship and Immigration Services, 2006).

> As many counseling and clinical psychology graduate students fear, I (TB) was not matched with an internship program the first year that I applied. This was really worrisome because my visa and I-20 expired the day after my internship would have ended had I completed my degree within the original time frame. Also, on a side note, I could only renew my Ohio driver's license up to the expiration date of my I-20. After I received my internship offer letter (proof of funding for the additional year), I applied for an extension of my I-20 and curricular practical training (to be authorized for employment for internship) through the Office of International Programs. As only one extension is granted, my advisor suggested an expected completion date in my application using the median time of program completion, as this would allow extra time for completion of my dissertation beyond my internship. The process went smoothly and I received my extension, curricular practical training authorization and, of course, my driver's license, with time to spare.

References

Columbia University International Programs and Services. (n.d.). *Coming to Columbia: Essential information for new international students.* Retrieved January 9, 2007, from http://www.columbia.edu/cu/isso/incoming/Coming_to_Columbia_for_Students.pdf

Kansas State University Lafene Health Services. (n.d.). *Frequently asked questions about: Tuberculosis and TB testing, Severe Acute Respiratory Syndrome and health insurance.* Retrieved March 1, 2007, from http://www.k-state.edu/lafene/intrnatlfaqs.htm

Michigan State University Physician's Office. (n.d.). *TB testing.* Retrieved March 1, 2007, from http://uphys.msu.edu/tbtesting/index.html

University of Maryland Baltimore County International Education Services. (n.d.). *Basic visa information for students in F-1 status.* Retrieved January 9, 2007, from http://www.umbc.edu/ies/ISS%20F1%20Status.html

University of Missouri-Columbia International Center. (n.d.). *Financial documentation requirements.* Retrieved March 1, 2007, from http://international.missouri.edu/isss/students-prospective/financial.shtml

University of Pennsylvania Office of International Programs. (n.d.). *Visa and immigration information.* Retrieved January 9, 2007, from http://www.upenn.edu/oip/iss/index.html

U.S. Citizenship and Immigration Services. (n.d.). *Visit the U.S.* Retrieved January 9, 2007, from http://www.uscis.gov/portal/site/uscis

U.S. Citizenship and Immigration Services. (2006, June 1). *Press release: USCIS reaches H1B cap.* Retrieved January 9, 2007, from http://www.uscis.gov/files/pressrelease/ FY07H1Bcap_060106PR.pdf

U.S. Department of State Bureau of Consular Affairs. (n.d.). *Exchange visitor (J) visas.* Retrieved January 9, 2007, from http://travel.state.gov/visa/temp/types/ types_1267.html

U.S. Department of State Bureau of Consular Affairs. (n.d.). *Student visas.* Retrieved January 9, 2007, from http://travel.state.gov/visa/temp/types/ types_1268.html

U.S. Department of State Bureau of Educational and Cultural Programs. (n.d.). *Exchange Visitor Program.* Retrieved January 9, 2007, from http://exchanges.state.gov/ education/jexchanges

U.S. Immigration and Customs Enforcement. (n.d.). *International Students.* Retrieved January 9, 2007, from http://www.ice.gov/sevis/students/index.htm

SOCIOCULTURAL ASPECTS OF LIFE IN THE UNITED STATES | IV

Olga Iof and Sandra M. Fowler

A Guide to Cultural Differences in the United States

7

I t is important for you as an international student to learn about and understand how culture influences behavior in the United States. Learning about American culture will enhance your educational experience and will assist you in establishing social support networks. Strong social support networks have been shown to increase the satisfaction with the overall educational experience of international students studying in the United States (Lin, 2000; Sam, 2001). Some aspects of American culture may be different from the culture that international students have experienced in their home countries. Indeed, you may find moving to the United States to be a difficult transition. In this chapter we provide information that can help international students develop a better understanding of American culture. Specifically, this chapter covers greetings, cultural misunderstandings, individualism, meeting others, social support, dress, language, classroom culture, social events, holidays, gender relationships, romantic relationships, and recreation.

Learning About American Culture

The ability to locate information about the culture of any country that you visit is an invaluable asset, especially during the first few months of being in this new environment. To facilitate a smooth transition to your new life, we recommend that you gather as much information about American culture as you can before you relocate. You can use television shows, movies, and Internet resources to collect information about life in the United States. Learning about American culture in this manner can be helpful, but it is important that you also use other methods. Other methods of gathering this information include visiting the local U.S. embassy, reading books and magazines about American culture, talking with an American citizen who may be working or studying in your home country, and communicating with a student who had a successful experience in the United States. You are also encouraged to contact universities and psychology programs to ask specific questions about local cultural norms.

Furthermore, there are many opportunities for you to learn about American culture after you arrive on campus. Trying to get to know and understand new acquaintances can be challenging. However, it is possible for you to begin to understand why people think and behave as they do. It is important that you recognize that the United States is a country with a large and heterogeneous population. Individuals in the United States are diverse in terms of race, gender, ethnicity, age, socio-economic status, religious beliefs, educational levels, and other variables. Although the United States has a heterogeneous population, there are several factors that you should be aware of regarding American cultural values and norms. The topics discussed in the following sections address common cultural factors that you may want to understand.

GREETINGS

The first cultural difference that you may notice is the way Americans greet each other. In the United States privacy is valued, so greetings may not be very intimate. For instance, in some cultures it is acceptable to greet another person with a kiss on the cheek regardless of gender, but in the United States people do not ordinarily kiss each other on the cheek. Greetings between students are usually informal, and some students prefer to use nicknames with their friends and acquaintances. Because of the individual differences among people, it is important that you observe how people in the region in which you are studying greet each other. It is also important that you ask questions about behaviors that are uncomfortable for you.

CULTURAL MISUNDERSTANDINGS

Sometimes cultural misunderstandings result from differences in communication style (Sue & Sue, 2003). In the United States the communication style is usually direct and linear (Fowler & Blohm, 2004), meaning that Americans typically state their points clearly and directly, and they use facts to justify specific points. They also focus on the words and not on the context of the communication. This is in contrast to people who prefer a more indirect style of communication that uses abstract stories to communicate a particular point. There will always be some situations in which misunderstandings are unavoidable. You should understand that it is unlikely that you will be able to prepare for all possible scenarios. To deal with any misunderstandings, you may want to inform others about your culture, values, and native country. A cultural misunderstanding may be smoothed over by talking to a third person who may help to clarify the situation. However, when the misunderstanding results in negative consequences, it is important that you consult with your advisor, supervisor, or program director to address the situation.

Citizens of the United States are proud of their country, specifically its political and economic advances. This patriotism may lead some American students to boast about their country's achievements to people from other nations (Althen, 1988). In these instances, some international students may feel that their own countries and cultures are not being respected. This is a legitimate feeling, and it is advisable to defuse any ill will by acknowledging other people's patriotic feelings and by sharing your own feelings of pride in your home country. This will help you develop new relationships with people in the United States, and it should help to lay the foundation for mutual understanding and acceptance of individual cultures.

INDIVIDUALISM

Many people in the United States respect the concept of uniqueness and value the rights of the individual (Sue & Sue, 2003; Triandis, 1994). Individualistic cultures such as the United States give a high priority to personal goals and define the self as a separate entity. Individuals from collectivistic cultures value group goals most highly and define the self in terms of membership in in-groups, such as family (Sue & Sue, 2003; Triandis, 1994). You are likely to find that students from the United States focus on their own needs, emotions, and independence. This approach may be challenging for international students who originate from collectivistic cultures. Thus, it is recommended that international students who experience difficulty with this concept of individualism consult with classmates, advisors, and supervisors about their concerns.

Nonetheless, the United States is a very diverse country, and there are many differences in customs and the degree to which people are individualistic (Sue & Sue, 2003). International students will encounter different traditions in different regions and with different ethnic and socioeconomic groups. Many students in the United States are proud of their ethnic heritage. These students will engage in rituals and celebrations handed down to them through family traditions. In addition, they may enjoy foods from other countries, foreign films, and literature from other lands.

MEETING OTHERS

International students are part of the college student subculture in the United States. There will be many opportunities for you to connect with classmates, professors, neighbors, and coworkers. You may find it easier to connect with other international students because of the common experience you share with them. However, you are also encouraged to become acquainted with people from the United States. When talking with American students, you should be open to exploring new opportunities and ideas, and you should be prepared to share your culture with others.

SOCIAL SUPPORT

Most universities have an international student advisor program that enables the advisors to learn what types of accommodation the university needs to make while also helping international students learn about the United States. Some international students will have choices about how much contact to have with American students, other international students, and students from their home countries. For instance, undergraduate students often live on campus, which provides many opportunities to make friends and learn about culture in the United States much more quickly. Graduate students, however, are more likely to live off campus. If you are a student who lives off campus, you may want to share an apartment with a roommate as this will not only help with expenses, but may also increase your opportunities for cross-cultural learning.

Additionally, you may find it helpful to connect with individuals from your native community and home country. If you live in a large city, you may be able to find a cultural center, neighborhood, or religious institution where you can find media, products, and events that are "just like home." Being among people with whom you share language and culture can be very comforting. It is also a good place to collect information about the United States from people whose values and perspectives you share. People in these communities have already gone through many adjustments and they may serve as mentors to international students. Local immigrant communities may also have access to and knowledge about services that cater to the needs of international students.

International students who live in small towns without immigrant communities may want to connect with immigrant communities online. The international office on campus may be able to provide helpful information about local resources. Many campuses have multicultural and interfaith centers where international students can interact with other students. However, if you find that you do not have many resources in your local area, you may want to take the initiative and start an international students association at your university.

DRESS

As an international student, you should think about how you will dress while you are living in the United States. Some students choose to wear their traditional clothes, and others may decide to wear clothes that reflect their adjustment to American culture. Regardless of the decision that you make, it is important that you wear clothes that make you comfortable. It is important to remember that there will be dress codes for specific events. For example, during a job interview, a person is expected to wear business-appropriate clothing. If you are not sure what to wear for a certain occasion, it is important that you ask a classmate or advisor for suggestions. If your cultural or religious beliefs do not allow you to wear certain garments, then you should wear clothes that are in line with your cultural beliefs. If you have concerns about how certain cultural or religious dress may be viewed, you should consult your advisor, supervisors, and classmates about your concerns. Consulting with others may help you avoid uncomfortable situations in which you are inappropriately dressed.

CLASSROOM CULTURE

Some international students may notice that classroom culture in the United States is different from the classroom culture and teaching techniques in their home countries. In this section we discuss two aspects of classroom culture. First, in the United States most professors expect that students will complete the assigned work on their own. Unless the professor states that collaborating with other students on an assignment is approved or expected, it is considered cheating. Cheating and plagiarism (which is quoting information without citing the source) are grounds for failing a course, and in some cases can lead to expulsion from the university (NAFSA: Association of International Educators, 1996; see also http://edupass.org/english/teaching.phtml). If you are unsure about what is considered cheating or plagiarism, you should consult with your instructors for guidance.

The second aspect to be addressed is class participation. In the United States, class participation is encouraged and sometimes it is a required part of the student's course grade. Participating in class may be challenging for international students who feel anxious about speaking English in front of the class. If you are having difficulty with class participation, you should talk with the class instructor and your advisor about these concerns. Instructors who teach international students may want to provide alternative ways (e.g., a written summary) in which these students can communicate their understanding of the class material. For more information about classroom culture in the United States, refer to chapter 10 of this book.

SOCIAL EVENTS

Although you are in the United States to further your education, being a student does not mean that you have to spend all your time studying. Socializing is an important part of the educational experience in the United States, as it is in many other countries. Students like to get together and have fun, and there will be many opportunities for you to meet new people and make new friends. It is not uncommon for the host of a large party to invite a few people who in turn invite their friends or partners. These individuals then invite their friends, and this pattern continues. This type of easygoing invitation process happens mostly, but not exclusively, at the undergraduate level. This informal and open process does not usually apply to formal dinners and official gatherings, to which guests receive personal or even written invitations. It is customary to bring small gifts to such a gathering.

You may also want to consider hosting your own party or a get-together with classmates. It would be a nice idea for you to invite classmates to share and get to know your culture. The party could include postcards or photos of your hometown, some traditional music, and traditional foods from your country. If you feel comfortable, you may even want to invite your classmates to partake in some of your cultural rituals.

HOLIDAYS

The United States celebrates many holidays throughout the year. Some holidays are considered federal holidays, which means that most government and some private businesses and organizations are closed (e.g., banks and post offices). Some universities may also be closed during federal holidays. A comprehensive list of holidays can be retrieved from the Internet at http://edupass.org/culture/holidays.phtml. During holidays, most people in the United States prefer to spend time with their families and friends. You may get an invitation from your classmates or advisor to participate in these celebrations. This is an excellent chance for you to learn about various American holidays, their traditions, and the reasons for them.

Some individuals in the United States celebrate ethnic or religious holidays that are not on the federal calendar. Many universities acknowledge the diversity among their student body, faculty, and employees and allow them to take days off for major religious holidays. Some universities even cancel classes to observe these holidays. These days are usually marked on universities' academic calendars. You may want to inform your advisor, classmates, and professors about the holidays that are important to you, especially if celebrating a holiday means that you will have to miss classes.

GENDER RELATIONSHIPS

Interpersonal behaviors are culturally learned, and different cultures endorse different kinds of relationship behaviors that are deemed appropriate (Triandis, 1994). In the United States equality between men and women is considered the norm, but this norm is not practiced by all American people. Some may experience equality between women and men in certain aspects of their life, but not in all. The debate about equality between men and women is long-standing and it is an issue that will continue to be discussed. As an international student, you will discover that gender relationships in the United States are complex and can vary depending on the social context.

International students need to examine the interpersonal behaviors that fit for them in their relationships. All cultures have both physical and emotional boundaries (The University of Akron Counseling, Testing and Career Center, 2007). Physical boundaries include issues such as physical space and touching. Emotional boundaries involve concerns such as feeling respected, being able to express opinions, and feeling comfortable with another person. Individuals from different cultures will differ in the way that they determine their boundaries. However, one signal that something in a relationship is not right is when an individual feels uncomfortable or unsafe with the physical space or the amount and kind of touching that is happening. If you feel uncomfortable or unsafe in any relationship, you should seek help from a trusted friend, advisor, or counselor.

Most people in the United States would agree that respect should be part of every relationship; this respect would include the freedom to express your opinions. However, your level of comfort in expressing your opinions might differ according to your relationship with your listener. You may feel differently about openly expressing your thoughts depending on whether you are speaking with your friends, family, roommates, classmates, professors, or employer. Most international students find they are less at ease sharing their opinions with professors and employers; that is to be expected. If you feel uncomfortable expressing yourself in any relationship, it is time to assess what might be causing your discomfort.

ROMANTIC RELATIONSHIPS

Establishing a romantic relationship is an important aspect of life. Some international students have to leave their significant others in their home countries as they study abroad, and others may find a partner while studying in the United States. Cross-cultural relationships can be both rewarding and challenging. International students who are interested in having a romantic relationship with an American may want to familiarize themselves with dating practices in the United States. Although there are no rules for dating, there are some important facts that international students should know.

Specifically, it is important that you are aware of some safety tips for dating if you decide to date in the United States (The University of Akron Counseling, Testing and Career Center, 2007). First, it is recommended that you introduce your dates to your friends. Second, in the beginning of a relationship it might be a good idea to invite your date to go out with you in a group of people or on a double date. Third, it is advisable to carry cash with you in case you need to leave and find your own transportation. Fourth, never leave your drink unattended at a party, because someone might add a drug to it. Fifth, it is important to know as much information as possible about the plans for the date, such as the location of the date (e.g., movie, park, or restaurant) and the activity (e.g., bike riding, studying). Sixth, if you have doubts or concerns about going out with someone, you should consult a friend or colleague about your concerns. Finally, it is essential that you know that there is nothing wrong with a firm, polite "no," even if the other person indicates he or she is offended.

At many universities, students have started to use new and technologically advanced methods to locate potential romantic partners. For instance, some university students have explored speed dating and online matching agencies to meet potential partners. Speed dating is an organized event at which single people can meet several potential partners in person and talk for a predetermined amount of time, such as 8 or 20 minutes. This type of dating allows single students to meet many people in a short amount of time, and it is usually organized by university student groups or community agencies. There are numerous online matching agencies, such as Match.com, which allow university students to create an electronic profile and meet potential partners through the Internet. However, many of these agencies require that you pay a fee to participate. These new dating methods are popular with some university students who are competent in electronic technology, who are seeking certain types of partners, and who may be having trouble meeting potential partners in their local area. Although these methods are popular, there are many issues to consider before using these types of dating methods. One issue of great importance is safety. Many online dating agencies provide specific recommendations for online dating safety. It is essential that international students who decide to use these methods follow those safety rules.

Furthermore, some international students may come from cultures in which dating is not a common practice. These students may want to make a decision about whether to maintain their traditions or follow the customs for dating in the United States. If you choose to refrain from dating, you may want to share this information with other people whom you trust. However, you should recognize that dating is very common in the United States, and that some individuals from the United States might view students who do not date as unusual. If you decide you do not want to date while you are studying in the United States, you may want to tell others that you are not ready for a relationship or that you prefer to meet someone from back home. A response like this is less likely to be perceived negatively.

RECREATION

You may have limited funds available for fun activities while you are studying in the United States. The high cost of education and the additional expenses placed on international students, such as visa fees and health insurance payments, may strain your budget. Despite limited funds, you should be able to enjoy various cultural events by locating free or inexpensive activities. You can learn about such events by reading local and university newspapers, exploring city Web sites, reading city guides, and asking people who are local residents of the area. Some inexpensive activities include visiting parks, attending community center events, attending university activities, participating in program functions, attending movies, and working out in the university or community gym.

Conclusion

There are many challenges, but also many rewards, involved in pursuing your studies in the United States. Understanding the culture of the United States is a challenging task because of the changing nature of culture and the diversity of the American people. It is important to persevere with understanding and accepting American culture if you want to accomplish your personal and educational goals while you are in the United States. Learning about American culture and how it influences values, customs, rituals, and relationships will help all international students develop the skills needed to succeed. When you return home, you will realize how much you have learned about yourself and about Americans as a result of your adventure.

References

Althen, G. (1988). *American way.* Yarmouth, ME: Intercultural Press.

Fowler, S., & Blohm, J. (2004). An analysis of methods for intercultural training. In D. Landis, J. Bennett, & M. Bennet (Eds.), *Handbook of intercultural training* (pp. 37–84). Thousand Oaks, CA: Sage.

Lin, J.-C. G. (2000). College counseling and international students. In D. C. Davis & K. M. Humphrey (Eds.), *College counseling: Issues and strategies for a new millennium* (pp. 169–183). Alexandria, VA: American Counseling Association.

NAFSA: Association of International Educators. (1996). *NAFSA's international student handbook: A guide to university study in the U.S.A.* Washington, DC: Author.

Sam, D. L. (2001). Satisfaction with life among international students: An exploratory study. *Social Indicators Research, 53,* 315–337.

Sue, D. W., & Sue, D. (2003). *Counseling the culturally diverse: Theory and practice* (4th ed.). New York: Wiley.

The University of Akron, Counseling, Testing and Career Center. (2007). *Gender relations in America: Negotiating healthy boundaries.* Akron, OH: Author.

Triandis, H. (1994). *Culture and social behavior.* New York: McGraw-Hill.

Sin-Wan Bianca Ho and Hsiao-Wen Lo

Sharing Your Culture $\Big|$ 8

The experience of being an international student is filled with excitement, frustration, challenges, and rewards. Cross-cultural interaction and the sharing of cultures is an inevitable part of the experience. As you encounter and experience the differences and similarities between your own culture and the host culture, you may find yourself alternating between the roles of learner, educator, and advocate, depending on the situation.

The sharing of cultures may be a common situation for international students; however, this process of sharing and understanding is not always as simple as it appears. In this chapter we discuss three important concerns involved in the type of cultural interaction you will experience when you study in the United States. First, the issues to consider before sharing one's culture are outlined. Second, the barriers to sharing are discussed, and finally, suggestions on how to effectively share your culture with others are presented.

Elements to Consider Before Sharing Your Culture

It is important to keep in mind that cultural sharing can be done in a conscious or unconscious manner. For example, people may be sharing or not sharing a part of their culture by what they eat or do not eat, what they wear or do not wear, what they say or do not say, and when they say or do not say it. They may not be consciously thinking about it, but they are sharing their culture with the person with whom they are interacting. In this chapter we focus on purposeful, and thus conscious, sharing.

There are several elements to consider when sharing your culture with others. The first element is the content of what is being shared. There is a wide range of topics you can share, including food, music, holidays, lifestyles, religions, beliefs, traditions, values, emotions, and perceptions. Some topics are more tangible than others (e.g., food vs. emotions) or more accessible through direct observation (e.g., behaviors such as eye contact vs. values such as respect). The second element is the context of what is being shared. The context for international students who are sharing their culture can be divided into academic and nonacademic contexts. Cultural sharing in the academic context may include class discussions, class presentations, written assignments, advisory interactions, and supervisory interaction. Nonacademic contexts are settings outside of academic areas, including interaction with your landlord, host family, and friends and acquaintances outside your academic program. The third element is the purpose of the cultural sharing. Some common reasons for international students to share their culture are the enhancement of mutual understanding and the resolution of conflicts.

An example of the different levels of cultural sharing that you might experience as an international student can be seen in the following example. In explaining his culture's accepted ritual of worshiping deceased grandparents, Mr. L describes the procedures and various food prepared for a ceremony he participated in with his family. The sharing experience deepens after he recalled the time that his father insisted that a certain kind of inexpensive sweet be present before the ceremony should begin. When Mr. L, a young child at the time, asked about the reason behind his father's insistence on this food, his mother explained that the sweet was his paternal grandmother's favorite. However, as Mr. L's family was on a tight budget, his grandmother rarely indulged herself, even with such an inexpensive treat. Mr. L's mother explained that this grandmother passed away at age 44 because of illness, and that Mr. L's father always regretted that his mother never enjoyed the improved qualify of life the family later achieved. Mr. L recalled that such a seemingly insignificant gesture, the buying of his grandmother's favorite candy, had left such a strong impression on him. For Mr. L, the sweet symbolizes his father's longing to express his love for his mother. Thus, depending on the purpose of the cultural sharing and the nature of the relationship between those participating, the sharing of cultures can be a matter of simple exchange of information, or it can be a much more human and emotional sharing. The story of this inexpensive sweet and what it meant to his family brought Mr. L's cultural sharing beyond that of the exchange of information about a ritual, and transformed it into a deeper sharing of family relationships and values.

OBSTACLES TO SHARING

Sharing your culture with others has significant implications for research, training, and clinical work. However, there are several obstacles that you may find inhibit the sharing of your culture. These obstacles include perceived confrontation, complexity of cultural differences, lack of experience or skills in cross-cultural communication, and previous unpleasant experiences you may have experienced in sharing your culture. In this section we discuss these obstacles and provide examples to clarify how they affect cultural sharing.

Perceived Confrontation

Sometimes international students may decide not to share cultural differences because they are concerned that it might be perceived as confrontation and not as sharing. For example, Ms. W may choose not to share how the educational system is different in her native country because she does not want her American classmates and professors to think that she is implying that the educational system in her country is better than the American educational system. Mr. O may choose not to share how uncomfortable it is for him when his American friends greet him with hugs because he wants to avoid appearing rude. Most international students are eager to acculturate and to fit in, and as a result they may choose not to share their differences in order to be accepted.

Complexity of the Cultural Difference

International students may choose not to share aspects of their culture because of the complexity of the cultural difference. Some cultural differences are easier to explain and articulate than others. For example, it is generally easier to explain differences that are easily understood and readily observable, such as behaviors, foods, and holidays; it is harder to explain differences that are intangible, such as attitudes and values. It is also easier to explain a custom, a behavior, or a value if there are equivalent words or expressions in English, which may not always be the case. Your confidence in your ability to articulate the differences and your decision on whether or not to share certain aspects of your culture with others may depend on how well you have mastered the English language and on how well you understand the differences in the cultural experiences.

Lack of Experience and Skills in Cross-Cultural Communication

Cross-cultural communication is a complicated process. Implicit and explicit messages can be transmitted through words, sounds, symbols, and gestures, whether or not the individual realizes that he or she is communicating these signals. When some individuals first encounter a cross-cultural context, they may not readily possess the skills necessary for effective communication; therefore, they may shy away from sharing. This may be true for some students and the individuals they come in contact with, including faculty, staff, classmates, clients, neighbors, and roommates. A lack of experience or skills in cross-cultural communication for one or both parties involved can create barriers to sharing.

Previous Unpleasant Experience

There may be times when students choose not to share in a given situation because they have had an unpleasant experience in a similar situation in the past. They may have been dismissed when attempting to share an aspect of their culture, treated with indifference when they shared, or been asked or felt coerced into conforming to the mainstream culture. For example, Mr. D shared with his class the differences in diagnosing certain psychopathology in the United States and in his country. After his contribution to the discussion, his instructor said, "Yes, but you are in the United States now" and proceeded on to the next topic. Mr. D felt that his comments were not welcomed, and he was disappointed about the missed opportunity for class discussion. Some international students may decide not to share examples from their culture because they feel that their fellow students may not be interested in cross-cultural interaction; this might not be related to the actions or comments of other students but may in fact be related to their own personality characteristics or ethnocentrism. Given that personality traits and values are not easy to change, international students may choose to not address this issue unless it is absolutely necessary.

SUGGESTIONS ON HOW TO SHARE YOUR CULTURE

As mentioned previously, sharing your culture is a challenging task because of the various elements of this type of communication and the barriers to expressing aspects of your culture. In this section we offer specific suggestions on cultural exchange that should help you to be prepared for situations when you would like to share your culture with others.

Be Open-Minded

It is helpful to keep an open mind, because experiencing cultural differences is inevitable when you are living in another country. However, although there may be differences between two cultures, one culture is not intrinsically better than the other. You may want to avoid comparing two cultures and imposing values on the differences, such as "good versus bad," "right versus wrong," "smart versus stupid," etc. It would be beneficial for you to value the opportunity of understanding and to appreciate the differences that you discover. Moreover, it can be frustrating when other people, particularly those who have not lived in another culture, cannot seem to understand or relate to the experience of culture shock. It is important not to assume that they are insensitive or do not care.

Assess the Context and the Relationship

One factor to consider when sharing your culture is formality. You may want to assess the context and the relationship to determine how formal your manner or communication style should be. For example, Ms. A may use a more formal approach when sharing with her advisor how a classroom discussion is not beneficial for her because of cultural differences; however, she may adopt a less formal approach when speaking with the advisor about cultural differences in how families spend time together during holidays.

Spontaneity is another factor to keep in mind. Cultural sharing during a casual, social conversation is generally more spontaneous than sharing aspects of your culture in a formal presentation. A presentation is more purposeful and requires varying levels of preparation or research. This is not to say that cultural sharing in a social conversation cannot be purposeful. After weighing the pros and cons of doing so, Mr. K may decide to bring up certain cultural issues during a social conversation with his colleague because he thinks that his colleague will feel more at ease discussing these concerns in a social setting.

Sharpen Cross-Cultural Communication Skills

You may want to take advantage of opportunities to improve your cross-cultural communication skills, which can often be improved by practicing communication in your everyday life as well by learning from the experience of others. Phrases such as "it seems as though we're misunderstanding each other," or "this may sound strange to you, but let me try and explain again," may be helpful in opening up the dialogue. You may also try saying "I noticed that you seem puzzled. Was it something I said or did? I didn't mean to offend you, but I may have said something offensive without intending to. Will you help me understand what is going on?"

In addition to communicating effectively in a cross-cultural encounter, you need to be sensitive to potential conflicts that may arise because of the interaction of different cultural practices. Having understanding and knowledge of your culture and the culture you are living in is helpful in identifying the cultural elements that happen during everyday encounters. Having the knowledge will certainly assist in communication. However, it is not always practical or possible for you to study all aspects of all cultures. Paying attention to the interaction or disconnection when it occurs will enhance the quality of the interaction or remediate problems promptly.

Manage Your Emotional Reactions

Cross-cultural communication can be frustrating if you find a particular interaction offensive to your beliefs or values. It is important to keep in mind that others may not intend to offend and may not even be aware that it is offensive. Being patient with yourself and others helps prevent an overly emotional reaction to such situations. It is easy to assume that you know another person's motivations and ideas, although you may not understand what they are trying to communicate. Unfortunately, assumptions about the motives of others are not necessarily accurate, especially in a cross-cultural setting. It is crucial to make an effort to notice when such assumptions are made and to discuss your concerns with someone who does not share your culture to avoid being misled by such assumptions. Instead of saying, "it's selfish of you to ask me to . . . ," you might try saying, "I was really surprised when you asked me to . . . Can you tell me more about why you asked?" Taking the time to talk about uncomfortable situations will help enhance mutual understanding.

It is also important to distinguish between someone's personal opinion and actual facts. A comment such as, "making direct eye contact when speaking to an elderly person feels inappropriate to me," sends a different message than a comment such as, "making direct eye contact when speaking to an elderly person is inappropriate." The former comment is stated as an opinion and represents the speaker's experience, which is an effective way of communicating the speaker's values and attitude. The latter comment is stated as fact and can be perceived as an imposition of the speaker's values on the listener. The speaker is entitled to the belief that making direct eye contact when speaking to an elderly person is inappropriate; however, stating it as a universal fact can be problematic in a cross-cultural setting. Thus, it is crucial to share opinions as opinions and facts as facts; mixing the two may create misunderstanding and friction.

Read About Literature on Cross-Cultural Interactions

Existing literature on cross-cultural studies provides abundant knowledge and information that may help you articulate the cultural differences you experience. You may be surprised that this literature points out how frequent and universal some of the experiences are. The literature could help you put your experiences in perspective and help you gain insight into how to better interact with students from the United States.

Be Persistent

It is not easy for anyone who is living in a new and culturally different country to openly share all aspects of his or her culture without any hesitation or reservations. The outcome of trying to be open and sharing may be determined by several factors, including the topics discussed, the level of interest in the information, and communication skills. It can be frustrating when the outcome is not as positive as you would like. It is important to remember that sharing your culture is a skill that can be learned and improved with practice.

Know That You Will Offend

Sooner or later, you will probably say or do something that will offend others. Be prepared for this. The goal is not to avoid all offenses, because they are inevitable. Rather, the goal is to be able to realize that an offense has taken place and to apologize for the offensive act. Use the cross-cultural communication skills to resolve the conflict and reach a mutual understanding.

Manage Your Stress and Culture Shock

Some common feelings you may have if you experience culture shock include annoyance, irritability, frustration, anger, disgust, lowered self-confidence, and confusion. These are normal reactions and feelings. There is no need to ignore or to magnify them. Be aware that these are the feelings that you are experiencing. They are indicators that something is going on within a given situation. It is also important to reflect on the situation. Seek support from your friends, colleagues, supervisor, and advisors.

Seek Support

Talk with other international students about your experience. It can be a relief if you find that you are not the only person to have these experiences and feelings. Exchanging experiences with other international students can help you overcome your feelings of isolation and decrease self-doubt.

Willingness to Learn, Forgive, and Let Go

It is important to remain open-minded about cross-cultural experiences and to be willing to learn from these situations. It is also important to forgive yourself and others if offenses are made. Learn from the situation and let go of the regrets.

Conclusion

In this chapter we outlined important factors for you to consider before sharing aspects of your culture. We identified potential obstacles that prevent international students from sharing their cultures and made suggestions on how to maximize the benefits of sharing and minimize negative outcomes, all of which should help you enjoy your experience of studying in the United States.

Yuhong He and P. Paul Heppner

Enhancing the Mentoring Relationship for International Graduate Students: Tips for Advisors and Advisees

9

I n 2005 there were approximately 565,000 international students studying in the United States (Open Doors 2005, 2005). As the American system of higher education is often quite different from the educational systems in other countries, many of the large number of international students studying in the United States typically experience new or different academic expectations, procedures, and learning environments. A key concern for a student who is pursuing graduate education in psychology in the United States is the mentoring relationship with his or her advisor. We acknowledge at the outset that there are many complexities in any mentoring relationship, and that the type and level of any mentoring relationship is often affected by various training philosophies across training programs, departments, and universities. In this chapter we provide general suggestions on how to enhance the mentoring relationship for international graduate students in psychology, keeping in mind all these complexities.

Suggestions for International Graduate Students

We suggest international students take an active role in enhancing their relationships with their advisors. There are a number of things students can do to increase their satisfaction with their mentoring relationship. First and foremost, international students should try to gain a better understanding of their advisors and themselves in their advisor–advisee relationships. In addition, it is important for students to be aware of the different phases of the mentoring relationship and the strategies that they can use at each stage.

KNOWING YOUR ADVISOR

For any advising relationship to work, it is essential that you understand who your advisor is as a person. You are encouraged to approach the advisor–advisee relationship with an open mind. It is crucial that you first understand what the boundaries and parameters are on your relationship with your advisor. As the relationship develops, it is important to try to understand your advisor's culture of origin, personal and professional identity, spirituality, and gender role expectations, which will enable you to understand and appreciate your advisor as an individual. Such knowledge tends to facilitate more effective communication between you and your advisor because you have developed a better sense of your advisor's strengths, limitations, boundaries, and expectation for his or her advisees. With this level and type of understanding, you may be able to avoid potential conflicts with your advisor. One way to gather this information is to ask your advisor directly about training expectations and about the type of relationship the advisor tends to build with his or her advisees throughout a training program. Another way is to ask other advisees for their perceptions of your advisor's stylistic and training philosophies; however, it is essential to remember that other advisees' perceptions can be affected by their personal and professional interests and needs.

UNDERSTANDING YOURSELF

It is also important that you are aware of your own worldview, cultural values, and communication style, and how these factors, in turn, affect your interactions and relationship with your advisor. In addition, we encourage you to reflect on and become aware of all the joys and challenges you are experiencing in the many new cultures in your life (e.g., program, department, university, state, and country). With all the transitions you are going through, you should remember that you have many personal strengths and a great deal of resilience, characteristics that have helped you achieve so much success. Such awareness and self-reflection can be helpful to you in understanding the cultural exchange inherent in an advisor–advisee relationship, and that this exchange will highlight the different styles and expectations that you both bring to the relationship. Sometimes international students and their advisors may have difficulty communicating with each other because of different assumptions related to language, culture, or personality differences. We encourage you and your advisor to continually consider your behaviors within your individual cultural context and to openly discuss issues that bring joy as well as challenges into the relationship. In addition, attending to an advisor's interest in international issues as well as a student's home culture and country provides additional information about the type of relationship that you may develop with your advisor.

DEVELOPMENTAL PHASES OF THE ADVISOR–ADVISEE RELATIONSHIP

You should be aware of three general time periods in building a good relationship with your advisor: the time prior to entering the program, during the program, and after the program.

Before Entering the Program

When students choose a graduate program in psychology, they often identify one or two faculty members who share similar professional interests. If you are an international student who is assigned an advisor prior to entering the program, you should note that the first step to building a good relationship is to contact your advisor as early as possible. An example of this contact would be e-mailing your advisor to discuss your feelings about entering the program and working with him or her (e.g., your feelings of excitement), as well as to ask if there are any expectations before you formally begin your program. In addition, we suggest that you share your relocation plan with your advisor. In other words, the relationship building process can begin even if you are thousands of miles away from your advisor.

During the Program

After beginning the program, you should initiate the first meeting to begin to develop a face-to-face relationship. In general, we suggest that you take advantage of your advisor's strengths and learn as much as you can from his or her expertise. We also encourage you to tell your advisor about your individual strengths and the unique challenges that you face as an international student. It is also important throughout the training program to maintain regular meetings with your advisor, to update him or her about your academic progress, and to seek advice on a wide array of professional and personal issues. To make the best use of these meetings, we suggest that you prepare in advance, prioritize discussion topics, and reflect on the discussion afterwards. In many instances, you can acquire varying levels of professional socialization into your chosen profession, such as information about practice and research. Depending on the advisor's mentoring style, these discussions can lead to collaborative opportunities in areas of mutual interest.

After the Program

After you complete your program of study, it is important to maintain a relationship with your advisor to receive guidance and mentoring as a young professional. It may also offer opportunities for you to continue to collaborate on a broad range of mutually beneficial projects. For international students who move back to their home countries to pursue their careers, previous advisors can become an important connection with the professional field in the United States, as well as a valuable resource for their career development.

Suggestions for Faculty

Faculty play a critical role in any advisor–advisee relationship and can provide international students and themselves with a more satisfying mentoring relationship by knowing their students and their cultures, recognizing students' strengths and stressors, helping students solve their problems, and being sensitive to international students' disadvantages and training needs.

GETTING TO KNOW THE STUDENT AND HIS OR HER CULTURE

It is commonly agreed that the relationship or the working alliance between a faculty member and a student is an essential component in advising and mentoring graduate students. Thus, it is very important to get to know advisees: who they are as individuals, their personal and professional interests, and their strengths and areas in which they need improvement. It is important to meet with them frequently to get to know them on a personal level and develop a relationship, and this may initially include meetings on a regular basis—perhaps as often as once a week.

In addition, the advisee–advisor relationship is a function of a number of factors, one of which is the need for each person to have empathy for the other. This is related to the ability of one person to understand the cultural context of the other, and subsequently understand the meaning of the events in that person's life within their cultural context. What this means for a faculty member is that he or she needs to have a certain amount of knowledge about a student's culture (and the student needs to have relevant information about the faculty member's culture and worldview). Thus, the faculty member may read about a student's culture, talk with the student about his or her culture, or even travel to that country to learn firsthand about the culture and environmental context. It can also be a rich experience for a faculty member to learn about different cultures and to broaden and enrich his or her worldview. By immersing themselves in another culture, faculty members will also be more likely to understand and have empathy for the situations and adjustments that international students experience when entering a new culture.

Furthermore, to understand and develop a relationship with an international advisee, it is essential to consider the advisee's statements, feelings, and behaviors within the student's cultural context, as opposed to the cultural context of the United States. This often means that the faculty member needs to ask more questions to understand the student's comments and reactions within his or her cultural context. Sometimes this means explicitly asking the student what a comment or situation means for him or her in the home culture. It is also important for a faculty member to be aware of the need to help inform advisees about his or her cultural context and worldview; this information can help students understand the comments and behavior of the faculty member.

UNDERSTANDING THE STUDENT'S STRESSORS AND RECOGNIZING STRENGTHS

International students may not only experience the normal stressors related with graduate school but will also experience acculturative stress related to the process of transitioning from one culture to another. Common acculturative stressors for students might relate to new and unfamiliar food, social customs, academic rules and regulations, discrimination related to being from another country, and speaking and writing in English. For example, a student may have done well academically in his or her home country but may find that after entering a new culture with different academic procedures, he or she is experiencing difficulty maintaining the same high level of academic performance. The student's performance may not meet his or her own expectations or parental expectations, which may lead to stress or feelings of shame related to disappointing his or her family. Or a student might have been a successful therapist in her or his home country but may have difficulty counseling clients in English and difficulty understanding American culture. This obviously would be quite a discrepancy for the student and could result in a great deal of stress and embarrassment. However, it is important to remember that international graduate students demonstrate tremendous courage and fortitude by leaving their home culture, familiar style of communication, support systems, food, art, and social lives to build a new life in an unknown land that has different rules and cultures. Through studying and conversing in a second language and dealing with a myriad of transitional issues, such as learning a new transportation system, learning routine transactions in retail stores (e.g., grocery stores), and generally doing well in graduate school, students show a tremendous amount of adaptability and resilience, which is important for faculty to recognize.

SUPPORTING THE STUDENT AND COLLABORATIVE PROBLEM SOLVING

Keep in mind that international students often miss the social support they are used to receiving at home, as they have usually left behind family, friends, and mentors. Social support buffers stress. We encourage faculty and advisors to communicate to a student that you are there to provide emotional and instrumental support to cope with her or his problems. In addition, all graduate students need advice and help with problem solving, from course selection, choosing internship sites, or mastering the art of a successful dissertation defense. We encourage faculty to provide such advice, as well as to be active problem solvers about any culturally related issues that the advisee may have. Sometimes an advisee may need information about issues related to the local or academic culture, such as the rationale behind particular rules.

RECOGNIZING TRAINING IMPLICATIONS OF THE STUDENT'S CAREER GOALS

In the past faculty typically trained graduate students to work in a predominately White culture in the United States. Training in psychology has gradually changed over the years to include a range of multicultural competencies aimed at working with diverse populations. We encourage faculty members to be aware of the training implications for an international student who plans to return to his or her home country. Will this mean that the training the student receives in the United States needs to be altered in either small or significant ways? If so, what types of discussions or training adjustments need to happen while the student is studying in the U.S. program? We strongly encourage faculty to have open discussions about these complex training issues with their advisees.

BEING AWARE OF RULES THAT DISADVANTAGE SOME STUDENTS

Rules are essential for any graduate training program. This often means treating everyone in the same manner. Sometimes when we try to follow the rules and treat everyone the same, we ignore important cultural differences or the cultural context of international students, which subsequently puts them at a distinct disadvantage. For example, a faculty member teaches a discussion-oriented class in which classroom participation counts as part of the course grade. International students, especially those who are just beginning their training, may experience more stress in speaking English (their second language) in this classroom setting. By expecting the same level of discussion from all students, this equal treatment may end in unequal consequences in terms of grades. Another example would be that of a faculty member who requires all practicum students to disclose their personal feelings in supervision. This may be more difficult for students who come from cultures in which such levels of personal disclosure to teachers is rare. In short, it is important to understand that cultural context differs across students, and that some course requirements or program expectations and rules result in unequal circumstances and unintended negative consequences. We encourage faculty to seek feedback on such issues to enhance their awareness of such unintended consequences.

CONFLICT RESOLUTION

When conflicts arise between an advisor and an international student, what can the student and faculty do? It is hard to identify specific guidelines for conflict resolution because the conflicts can range from isolated, small issues to repeated and large conflicts. Conflict resolution also differs greatly depending on the people involved, their personalities, worldviews, cultural backgrounds and norms, styles of coping with stressful events, cross-cultural competencies, and comfort levels in dealing with conflict. In addition to the power differentials in the relationship, the conflict is also embedded within a host of issues between the student and faculty member (e.g., length of the relationship, level of perceived safety, strength of the working alliance, communications style, level of previous disclosure and honesty, etc.). There are many factors that affect the ability of the advisor and advisee to resolve conflict in their relationship.

We first remind both international students and faculty that it is normal to experience negative feelings such as frustration, confusion, and helplessness in the middle of conflicts, as well as during much of the course of a cross-cultural relationship. We understand that some students may even feel paralyzed about having conflicts with their advisors because they perceive their advisors as main support resources in the United States, a place they generally receive less social support than in their home countries. In general, we encourage students and faculty to try to resolve the conflict while maintaining awareness of the cultural backgrounds and interpersonal styles of each person. After all, the advisee–advisor relationship is one of the most important training relationships for students, and maintaining a strong mentoring relationship is usually helpful for most students.

When conflicts arise, we encourage international students and faculty to slow down and reflect on the situation, especially when they experience strong emotional reactions. Both parties should try to recognize the messages behind their emotions, reassess the situation from different perspectives, think about the statements or actions of each other within a cultural context, and find a good opportunity to communicate thought processes and feelings to each other. It is incumbent on faculty members to be aware of the inherent power differential in this relationship and also to be aware of their primary role as a teacher. Likewise, it is incumbent on students to be aware of the power differential, remember that they are in training, and accept their status as newcomers to the culture and the training environment and norms.

To help students and faculty objectively evaluate a situation and develop ideas on how to handle it, each may share their feelings with people they can trust (e.g., families, friends, mentors, and therapists). Students might also consult other faculty or fellow students, especially other international students, perhaps by using hypothetical scenarios. It is critical that the student be aware that peers and other faculty members can provide new insights and perspectives but can also offer misinformation, personal biases, and bad advice. In short, we encourage students and faculty to discuss concerns about their relationship with each other, because open communication will help both the advisor and advisee better understand the other's position. It will also reduce misunderstandings that may come from different worldviews, assumptions, and communication styles. By directly addressing the disagreement, the relationship between the advisor and the international advisee can be healthier and may last longer.

Students have different comfort levels in directly confronting their advisors, and we respect all students' ways of coping with conflicts that are in line with their cultural values and practices. However, it is important that students be aware of cultural differences and also aware of how cultural styles (e.g., indirect communication) might affect the resolution of the conflict. Students should also think about how their behavior might be misperceived by an advisor with a different worldview (e.g., the indirect communication may be seen as untrustworthy). We want to emphasize, however, that international students have equal rights to educational opportunities and are entitled to voice their concerns in an academic setting.

Conclusion

Every relationship is different, and this truth applies to the advising and mentoring relationship between advisors and international advisees. There are many ways to approach an advisor–advisee relationship for international student populations from different countries, as well as for faculty from different cultural backgrounds across different training programs. Thus, this chapter is not intended to cover the entire constellation of factors that could facilitate a good advisor–advisee relationship. Instead, we hope our discussion might motivate faculty members and international advisees to think about their relationships and to consider the important cultural and individual factors that both parties bring to the relationship. We also hope our suggestions might inspire students and faculty to develop a truly successful and meaningful mentoring relationship. After all is said and done, the mentoring relationship might be one of the most important training outcomes for both students and faculty.

Reference

Open Doors 2005. (2005). *Open doors 2005: International students in the United States*. Retrieved December 12, 2007, from http://opendoors.iienetwork.org/?p=69736

ACADEMIC DEVELOPMENT | V

Anca Mirsu-Paun and Carolyn Zerbe Enns

The International Student in the Classroom: Teaching Others and Being Taught

10

A ccording to a report from the Council of Graduate Schools (2007) 13% of all graduate students in the United States are international students. Twenty-six percent of these international graduate students (IGSs) fund their studies through U.S. college or university sources (Institute for International Education [IIE], 2007), and many are commonly appointed as teaching assistants (TAs) or graduate assistants (GAs). In addition, university professors should expect to teach IGSs, particularly in fields such as business and management, engineering, and physical and life sciences, in which the percentages of IGSs studying in these departments are 17.8%, 15.3%, and 8.9%, respectively (IIE, 2007). In psychology graduate programs, IGSs represented an average of 3.6% of the total graduate student population during the 2006 through 2007 year (IIE, 2007). In some psychology programs such as the UCLA and American University, however, the percentage of IGSs was as high as 8% and 14%, respectively (UCLA Graduate Division, 2007; GradProfiles, 2007).

International students are usually referred to as a single category of students yet they represent a heterogeneous group. Their individual experiences in U.S. college and university classrooms may vary greatly, because of factors such as (a) similarities and differences between their countries of origin and the United States, (b) ethnicity, (c) age, (d) native language and English proficiency, (e) prior learning experiences within Western educational systems, and (f) social support network. In this chapter we address three main topics relevant to this diverse group of students: cultural variations in learning and classroom structures, accent and language concerns, and teaching techniques.

Cultural Variations in Learning and Classroom Structures

The following sections discuss potential cultural differences that might affect the interactions between instructors and graduate students and introduce effective modalities for dealing with these differences.

TEACHING AND LEARNING STYLES

North American educational practices typically emphasize independent thinking, exploration, analysis, and synthesis (Ladd & Ruby, 1999). In contrast, many international students may be accustomed to classes that involve class lectures, note taking, and memorization, rather than the public expression of personal ideas and opinions. Consequently, some students may feel uncomfortable participating in class discussions because people from their home cultures consider it inappropriate to publicly question professors and other people in authority. This hesitancy may place IGSs in a disadvantageous position in classes that require active participation. Consider the following student's experience, which summarizes some of the challenges of contributing to classroom discussion:

> Although my colleagues seemed to greatly enjoy carrying extensive class discussions, it was quite difficult for me to formulate and express opinions of my own. I doubted the value of my thoughts, and I felt that I did not have sufficient experience to make a significant contribution to class discussions. Fortunately, my class instructors were sensitive to the fact that I was an international student and they gently invited me to participate by asking for my opinion without making me feel obliged to speak as much as my colleagues. At times I also felt unsatisfied with the limitations of my verbal expression in English, and I was left wondering whether my colleagues and professors could understand my thoughts. The most frustrating experience was seeing people politely nod as though they "got" my ideas, even when they did not seem to completely understand what I was trying to say. It was more helpful when people asked directly for clarification if they were unsure what I was trying to communicate.

As the previous narrative illustrates, important behaviors for overcoming potential classroom obstacles include patience, understanding, encouragement, and the willingness to ask for clarification when meanings and intentions are unclear.

CULTURAL KNOWLEDGE AND RELATIONSHIP ISSUES

Because of a lack of shared cultural knowledge, IGSs may experience difficulties connecting with undergraduate students and even with graduate colleagues and professors. For example, IGSs may not be familiar with specific culture-based information, such as the role of student social organizations (e.g., sororities and fraternities) on American university campuses, or the importance placed on college football. In addition, they may be confused by slang, colloquial expressions, and references to culturally specific events (Collingridge, 1999). Some ways in which international students can increase their cultural knowledge include joining a student club, attending student events on campus, or participating in volunteer work for a few hours a week. These opportunities to interact with American students can also help IGSs improve their English skills and expand their social support network (Poyrazli, 2005).

Relationships between students and teachers in the United States vary, but are often less formal than in many other countries. For example, although it is not unusual for U.S. graduate students to call their professors by their first name, this practice is not typical in many other countries. The formal definition of the professor–student relationship held by many international students may contribute to their uneasiness about attending office hours or their limited awareness regarding the benefits of office hours. Office hours provide an excellent opportunity for students and their professors to learn more about each other (research interests, country of origin, etc.), and attending office hours allows students to show interest in classes, ask questions, and clarify assignments, exams, or class expectations (Poyrazli, 2005).

THE ROLE OF TEACHING ASSISTANTS

In contrast to many other countries, graduate TAs play an important role in U.S. universities. Their duties usually include teaching, grading assignments and tests, assisting individual students, and completing administrative work. International graduate students should consider their TAs as important resources because TAs are very knowledgeable about course content. TAs are usually approachable because they are also students, and they may be international students as well.

Language Concerns

The following section addresses issues specifically related to language concerns among IGSs, whether students or instructors.

VERBAL FLUENCY

Although international students are often required to pass language tests such as the Graduate Record Examination and the Test of English as a Foreign Language as part of their graduate application process, international students from non-English-speaking countries may not speak English fluently when they arrive in the United States. Many universities also require potential teaching assistants to take a test of spoken English. This test may require verbal answers to specific questions, which are often scored for accent thickness, word choice, fluency of speech, and ability to express complex ideas in English. Test fees are paid by international students from their own funds, and test scores are used to determine whether international graduate instructors should enroll in an academic English class. Although a rare occurrence, graduate international students are sometimes denied teaching assignments in their first semester because of their level of proficiency in spoken English. This outcome may create problems for students whose graduate funding is based on a teaching assistantship. (See chaps. 2 and 3 for additional information.)

WRITING SKILLS

International students may find the requirements to communicate in academic written English an obstacle, especially if they take classes with a paper-based evaluation system. This difficulty may not be indicative of their writing abilities, but is often related to having limited formal training that emphasizes mastery of English writing skills. Collingridge (1999) suggested that instructors should give honest grades but talk with international students about modalities for improvement. For example, one such modality is to ask a native English speaker to proofread papers and provide constructive feedback.

General Teaching Techniques

The first two topics in this chapter focus on general issues encountered by students and graduate assistants; however, this third and final section provides concrete advice for IGSs about classroom teaching practices. It summarizes 11 practical considerations for international instructors teaching in the U.S. undergraduate or graduate classroom.

MAKE USE OF TEACHING RESOURCES

Excellent teaching resources are available at most universities and may include classes and instructional technology workshops on diverse topics such as creating a Web page and syllabus online, multimedia presentations, entering student grades online, and antiplagiarism practices. A variety of Web sites are also devoted to the specific needs of beginning teachers and graduate assistants.

COLLECT MATERIALS RELEVANT TO TEACHING

As you attend academic conferences, you should consider how the content of conference presentations can be used to enrich teaching. Keep all written materials, flyers, PowerPoint presentation files, descriptions of interesting learning activities, or any other information from classes, conferences, or workshops. These materials, including those that are not directly related to teaching, may be invaluable resources for ideas and information about teaching.

In addition, you should attend as many presentations as possible on the teaching of psychology. The Society for the Teaching of Psychology (STP) provides exceptional conference programming on teaching and supports the Office of Teaching Resources in Psychology, which sponsors an extensive Web site of syllabus materials, teaching ideas, ancillary materials, and downloadable e-books about teaching (see http://www. teachpsych.org).

LEARN HOW TO INTERACT WITH PUBLISHING COMPANIES

Graduate instructors are typically responsible for choosing one or more textbooks and will usually need to interact with publishing companies. There are a few points you should keep in mind as you navigate through this process, including: (a) major textbook publishing companies assign representatives to each university and college department; (b) representatives' contact information can be found on the Web sites of publishing companies; and (c) publishing companies will send free textbooks for your perusal with the hope that you decide to use their texts. You are not obligated to adopt a text solely because you received an instructor's (free) copy (you have the right to decide not to use that particular textbook). As you negotiate with a publishing company representative, it is useful to ask whether there are any ancillary materials and classroom aids such as video materials, classroom activities, and test question banks that are available on request or adoption of a text.

PREPARE TO TEACH UNFAMILIAR MATERIAL

You may be assigned to teach unfamiliar courses, especially if your undergraduate degree was completed in your home country, in which the curriculum may be different than in the United States. Decisions about teaching assignments are typically made at a departmental level and graduate students have limited control over which courses they teach. Expressing a preference for one class over another is usually an acceptable practice and advocating for yourself may increase the likelihood of teaching a class that matches your expertise and interests.

SEEK SUPPORT, BUT PREPARE TO TEACH AUTONOMOUSLY

Procedures for monitoring GA and TA activities vary from one department to another, and IGSs can expect to receive a similar amount of guidance and supervision as their American colleagues. Overall, graduate TAs and GAs receive limited preparation prior to entering the classroom, may be given little or no supervision, and are often asked to perform many of the same duties as a faculty instructor (Branstetter & Handelsman, 2000). Although autonomy is a useful survival skill, finding mentors is also important. If you are unable to find organized institutional resources, you may consider forming an informal support group that focuses on sharing insights about teaching effectively. When face-to-face mentoring is unavailable, the online mentoring system of STP is also an excellent option.

USE CLASSROOM TECHNOLOGY

Various visual and audio methods (e.g., videos and PowerPoint presentations) are helpful because they enhance verbal communication with visual cues, illustrate major teaching points, help class instructors structure the presentation of material, facilitate student learning through the use of different modalities, and enhance the appeal of course material for students. Universities typically offer employees and graduate students opportunities to register for free workshops on using media tools and teaching technology. Such workshops are especially useful for identifying optimal forms and the quantity of information to include on tools such as PowerPoint presentations, as well as considering when such bells and whistles may allow students to become passive, rather than active and engaged, learners.

CHOOSE A PREFERRED TITLE AND REMEMBER STUDENT NAMES

When preparing to teach, you should consider how you would like students to address you (e.g., by first name, last name, a combination of Mr./Ms./Mrs. and first name, etc.). Expressing in a clear way a preference regarding names and title early in a class term makes it easier for students to know how to address and approach the class instructor.

Remembering the names of your students may be optional and a matter of personal choice in large classes. In addition, American names may be very different from the names used in your home country and may be difficult to learn. However, remembering student names can help you establish a connection with students quickly and easily. Even if you are not completely successful with learning their names, students are likely to appreciate the effort. Asking your students to state their names each time they address you may facilitate your remembering their names.

ESTABLISH AND MAINTAIN CONNECTIONS WITH STUDENTS

As you begin teaching, you may feel self-conscious about your use of English. Especially during the first few class sessions, you should speak as clearly and distinctly as possible. As students become familiar with the tone and style of your language patterns, you may be able to adopt a more relaxed speech style. You may also have difficulty understanding some of the speech patterns of your students (e.g., their questions or answers to discussion questions). In such cases, it is appropriate to ask students to repeat a question or response. After answering students' questions, you may ask whether they understand the answers or have any follow-up questions. International TAs or GAs can also increase clarity and maintain students' attention by supplementing verbal communication with facial expression, tone and pitch of voice, gestures, and consistent eye contact.

You can facilitate positive teacher–student relationships by encouraging your students to ask questions outside of class hours or by inquiring about students' interests that extend beyond the specific class content. You may also offer guidance to undergraduate students who have questions about graduate school admissions or who want to participate in research or volunteer activities that will broaden their experience. According to Martin and Hammer (1989), interpersonal skills are significant predictors of students' perceptions of teaching effectiveness. When international teachers who were equally proficient in language skills were evaluated by American students, the instructors with superior interpersonal skills were perceived to have superior language skills as well.

INCREASE EXPERIENTIAL LEARNING ACTIVITIES

A wide range of classroom activities can be used to enhance active learning, including role plays, class discussions, selections from well-known movies, group projects, illustrations based on movie and book characters, guest speakers, and other class exercises. Undergraduate teaching assistants can help develop creative and unique teaching activities and often have a good sense of what works in the teaching process because they can identify with the students in the class.

In addition to consulting the many books and Web sites that feature experiential learning options, you may make a unique contribution to active learning by including activities based on American Psychological Association task force recommendations for internationalizing the undergraduate curriculum (Lutsky et al., 2005). Nelson (1992) found that the use of personal cultural examples not only improves student perceptions of international teaching assistants but also enhances student recall of the class material.

LEARN HOW TO DEAL WITH CHALLENGING STUDENTS

Most graduate instructors have experienced at least one difficult student in their classes (e.g., a student talking during the lecture, making inappropriate comments, or asking the instructor for favoritism). You may feel less prepared than your American counterparts to deal with such students, especially if this type of student is rare in academic settings in your home country. It is important that you avoid taking personal responsibility for unexpected events and recognize that teaching activities can present challenges for all graduate students. It is helpful, however, to prepare for some potential situations. Other helpful strategies include consulting with faculty supervisors and asking other colleagues about their experiences with challenging students.

PREPARE FOR EVALUATION

It is a good practice to start thinking about your final evaluation at the beginning of the semester and to attend to students' needs for clarity, structure, challenge, and help throughout the term. Possible evaluation criteria include description of course objectives and assignments, communication of ideas and information, expression of expectations for performance in class, availability to assist students in or out of class, respect and concern for students, stimulation of interest in the course, and facilitation of learning.

Conclusion

We note that the personal experiences of the first author (Anca Mirsu-Paun) as an IGS should help other international students realize that it is helpful to (a) recognize the real challenges that many IGSs face and to approach these challenges gradually; (b) take advantage of opportunities to learn by doing; (c) ask for information, advice, help, and support when it is needed; (d) persevere in completing important goals; and (e) follow personal interests and passions as much as possible in the process.

References

Branstetter, S. A., & Handelsman, M. M. (2000). Ethical beliefs, behaviors, and training of graduate teaching assistants. *Ethics and Behavior, 10*(1), 27–50.

Collingridge, D. S. (1999). Suggestions on teaching international students: Advice for psychology instructors. *Teaching of Psychology, 26*(2), 126–128.

Council of Graduate Schools. (2007). *Findings from the 2007 CGS International Graduate Admissions Survey. Phase II: Final applications and initial offers of admission.* Retrieved December 9, 2007, from http://www.cgsnet.org/portals/0/pdf/R_IntlAdm07_II.pdf

GradProfiles. (2007). *American University.* Retrieved December 9, 2007, from http://www.gradprofiles.com/american.html

Institute for International Education. (2007). *Open doors 2007. Report on international educational exchange.* Retrieved December 9, 2007, from http://opendoors.iienetwork.org/?p=113124

Institute of International Education. (2007). *Open Doors 2007. Fast facts.* Retrieved December 9, 2007, from http://www.opendoors.iienetwork.org/file_depot/0-10000000/0-10000/3390/folder/58653/Fast+Facts+2007+Final.pdf

Ladd, P., & Ruby, R., Jr. (1999). Learning style and adjustment issues of international students. *Journal of Education for Business, 74*(6), 363–368.

Lutsky, N., Torney-Purta, J., Velayo, R., Whittlesey, V., Woolf, L., & McCarthy, M. (2005). *American Psychological Association Working Group on Internationalizing the Undergraduate Psychology Curriculum: Report and recommended learning outcomes for internationalizing the undergraduate curriculum.* Washington, DC: American Psychological Association.

Martin, J. N., & Hammer, M. R. (1989). Behavioral categories of intercultural communication competence: Everyday communicators' perceptions. *International Journal of Intercultural Relations, 13,* 303–332.

Nelson, G. L. (1992). The relationship between the use of personal, cultural examples in international teaching assistants' lectures and uncertainty reduction, student attitude recall, and ethnocentrism. *International Journal of Intercultural Relations, 16,* 33–52.

Poyrazli, S. (2005). International students at U.S. universities: Overcoming the challenges. *Eye on Psi Chi, 9*(2), 18–19.

UCLA Graduate Division. (2007). *Program report: Psychology.* Retrieved December 9, 2007, from http://209.85.165.104/search?q=cache:_CCEUb9W9LgJ:www.gdnet.ucla.edu/asis/progprofile/result.asp%3Fselectmajor%3D780+ucla+percent+ international+students+psychology&hl=en&ct=clnk&cd=1&gl=us

Yu-Wei Wang, Arpana Gupta, and Georgia T. Chao

Conducting Research in the United States

11

C onducting research is a competency that must be adequately developed and demonstrated in graduate education in psychology. Whether your career goal lies in academia or practice, it is crucial that psychologists understand how to critically evaluate existing research, build a successful research program, and identify future research needs. Conducting research in the United States can be an anxiety-provoking task for graduate students in general and for international students in particular. Some of the challenges surrounding research that are commonly experienced by all graduate students include identifying research topics, working with advisors and committee members, and writing literature reviews. Yet other challenges are especially pertinent to international students, such as unfamiliarity with the academic system and research environment in the United States, a lack of available mentors, uncertainty about career path (i.e., whether to remain in the host country, return to the country of origin, or go to a third country), language barriers, and insufficient research networks and connections (e.g., a paucity of sources for data collection).

Research Foundations and Overcoming Obstacles to Success

There are many helpful resources provided by individual institutions (e.g., guidelines for preparing theses and dissertations, writing centers, statistical consultants) that can assist with the issues common to all graduate students who conduct research in psychology. The goal of this chapter is to address the unique challenges facing international students in conducting research and to provide general suggestions for overcoming these obstacles. Specifically, practical tips for building a foundation for research, conducting a thesis or dissertation, seeking additional research experiences, presenting and publishing research, as well as obtaining research funding are presented. Relevant publications and Web sites on research advice and funding are listed in Appendix B at the end of the book.

BUILDING A FOUNDATION FOR CONDUCTING RESEARCH

Coursework

Graduate coursework in psychology is designed to provide a common knowledge base for all psychologists. In most programs and in all American Psychological Association (APA)-accredited doctoral programs in psychology, this includes courses in research design and statistical analyses. It is critical to develop competencies in these areas because conducting good empirical studies that merit publication in peer-reviewed journals often requires expertise in the latest research design and data analytic methods. It is also worth mentioning that not all psychology programs in the United States offer comprehensive training in qualitative inquiry (Ponterotto, 2005), despite the calls for methodological diversity (APA Presidential Task Force on Evidence-Based Practice in Psychology, 2006; Heppner, Casas, Carter, & Stone, 2000) and the increasing popularity of qualitative methodology within psychology and in many countries (Wang, 2008). International students who are interested in this research methodology can seek additional training opportunities by taking online courses, becoming involved in qualitative research teams led by faculty members in individual academic institutions, attending professional conferences on qualitative inquiry, or signing up for electronic mailing lists that are devoted to discussions on qualitative methodological issues (e.g., Forum Qualitative Sozialforschung, 2007). You are also encouraged to plan your curriculum around research content areas that are of interest to you. By taking courses in your areas of interest, you can start reviewing the relevant literature and develop potential research questions about different topics. Faculty members who teach these courses may be willing to serve as research supervisors or committee members for theses or dissertations.

Role Models and Mentors

Role models and mentors can help new students learn the skills needed to discuss research ideas with others and to function well on research teams. Role models and mentors may be faculty members or advanced graduate students. They form a developmental network for students and provide diverse models for conducting research. At the beginning of your graduate education, you should focus on building research skills rather than on leading research projects. Collaborative research projects involve teamwork and in an ideal situation, all points of view are equally valued. However, a new (particularly international) graduate student is entering an environment that already has established cultural norms of behavior. Thus, it may be to your advantage to learn how research teams operate, what is valued, and who has the power to influence research teams before you take a leadership position. If you are experiencing culture shock and adjustment issues, you also can benefit from having a faculty or peer mentor who can help you make sense of your new environment quickly and effectively. In sum, by helping others on their research, international students can learn about the research process and how psychologists conduct research in different ways. This information can be used to guide an international student's decisions about which areas to investigate and with whom to work on research projects.

THESES AND DISSERTATIONS

Most graduate programs in psychology require a thesis or dissertation that involves the design and conduct of original research with the help of an advisor and committee. Students typically complete a thesis for a master's degree and a dissertation for a doctoral degree. Requirements for a dissertation are often higher than those for a thesis. Therefore, a master's thesis may be a replication or modification of existing research, whereas a dissertation should contribute significantly to the existing literature. The advisor, or chair of the committee, serves as the main faculty member who supervises a student's thesis or dissertation and the rest of the committee generally serves in an advisory capacity. In programs that adopt the traditional mentoring model, advisors usually serve as the thesis or dissertation chairs; however, in other programs students have a primary advisor but may invite another faculty member to serve as the chair after choosing a thesis or dissertation topic. To avoid confusion, the faculty member who chairs a student's thesis or dissertation committee will be referred to as the thesis or dissertation advisor. Following are specific recommendations for conducting theses and dissertations.

Choosing Your Thesis or Dissertation Topics

Selecting your research topic is a creative, challenging, and exciting process. You are advised to consider several factors when choosing your topic:

personal passion, analysis of the current literature, level of research skills and experience, and your thesis or dissertation advisor's research expertise and interests. Specifically, the need to develop your own program of research (e.g., conducting your thesis and dissertation in the same research area) or particular research skills (e.g., learning how to construct a scale), the potential contribution to future research and practice, the need to meet societal needs, and the feasibility of the project (e.g., available time and resources, accessibility of the participant pool) may affect the selection of the research topic. A thesis or dissertation advisor can be most helpful if she or he has expertise in the research area that interests you. Talking to experts and reflecting on your own applied experiences also can help you formulate research ideas (Heppner & Heppner, 2004).

International students often encounter additional challenges in the process of selecting research topics. Sometimes students would like to conduct their theses or dissertations in their home countries or they may choose certain research topics because they intend to return home after graduation and hope to devote their research to addressing specific societal needs in their countries of origin. However, not all international students would be able to find thesis or dissertation advisors who have experience conducting research with international populations or are interested in these topics (Wang, 2006). You may want to discuss these issues with your mentor or advisor (or other senior international students) and brainstorm ways to accommodate your career goals and optimize your advisor's contribution.

Working With the Thesis or Dissertation Advisor and Committee

A poor working relationship with their thesis or dissertation advisor and committee is one of the major factors that prevent students from successfully completing their thesis or dissertation study (Heppner & Heppner, 2004; Wang, 2006). If you and your advisor do not share the same cultural background, cross-cultural miscommunications may occur. This makes it imperative that faculty and advisees understand each other's communication and work styles and clearly communicate what roles and responsibilities each person (including the committee members) has in the process of completing a thesis or dissertation (Lin, Shen, & Wang, 2006). It is important for you to consult with your thesis or dissertation advisor about how to choose, invite, and work with committee members, because a supportive committee is far more likely to encourage and guide a student's work, unlike a committee composed of members who do not share research perspectives or whose personalities clash.

You need to be aware of the thesis or dissertation deadlines set by departments or graduate schools for a particular graduation date. It is often helpful to generate a detailed and realistic timeline with the advisor. Such a timeline can include deadlines for finalizing the research topic and for revising and polishing drafts, as well as the amount of time that the advisor and committee need to read drafts and provide feedback. The time needed to complete a thesis or dissertation study depends on a myriad of factors, such as the type of research design, a student's prior knowledge about the subject matter, previous research experiences and skills, the amount of time that a student can devote to the research during regular academic semesters, as well as anticipated or unexpected problems encountered during the data collection or analysis process. International students whose first language is not English may have to devote more time to reading and writing articles in English. Therefore, the literature review and actual writing process may take much longer for them than for native English speakers. You and your advisor should be mindful of this challenge and plan the writing schedule accordingly.

If you need more structure, you may benefit from meeting regularly with your advisor to discuss your progress. You should keep in mind that faculty members are busy with other commitments and responsibilities; sometimes the advisor's schedule will not accommodate major changes in your research plan. It is unrealistic and unprofessional to give faculty members little turnaround time for feedback for you to meet your thesis or dissertation deadlines. Therefore, you should make every effort to stick to the proposed timeline. You can help ensure consistent progress by turning in drafts on time, incorporating feedback from advisors, and being prepared for meetings with specific questions (Lang, 2007).

Although you should try your best to produce good drafts for faculty review, those drafts are not expected to be perfect. In fact, research and writing both involve a nonlinear and evolving process, and advisors are expected to provide students with feedback on multiple drafts and research designs. Regular and open communication between you and your advisor is essential in this process. Soliciting honest and constructive feedback from faculty will not only enhance the quality and integrity of the research but will also contribute to your growth as a researcher and scientist. Remember that the thesis or dissertation is an academic exercise designed to teach students how to conduct research independently. Therefore, you should view each stage of the process, as well as the feedback, as an opportunity to learn and refine important research skills.

Literature Review and Language Issues

A literature review extends your knowledge base in a specific research area. A good literature review communicates what is currently known about a topic (content domain), how confident researchers are with current research findings (critiques of the literature), and how future research can contribute to the field's existing knowledge base. It is important to learn how to conduct a good literature review because the knowledge gained from the review helps define a person's expertise and can guide your future research program.

Most university libraries offer tours and additional help accessing library resources for a literature review. Some libraries even have librarians with specialized knowledge about various disciplines available to help their patrons. Online as well as on-site resources should be used for a thorough literature review. Also, international students often have the added advantage of being bi- or multilingual and can access literature published in English and other languages. In general, articles for a literature review should be evaluated for their technical merit as well as their content. Suggestions about methods of organizing and writing literature reviews can be found in Appendix B.

Reading and writing about numerous articles in English can be both intimidating and exhausting for international students whose first language is not English. Therefore, it is critical that you understand your own work style and observe how you cope with this type of pressure. You may procrastinate under stress (e.g., start other tasks, such as cleaning the house or surfing the Internet, rather than writing the literature review). Good self-care practices (e.g., physical exercise and meditation) and moral support from academic peers may help you deal with the stress you feel. You should keep in mind that the consequences of chronic procrastination may be grave, because your length of stay in the United States is restricted by visa and immigration regulations.

Research has indicated that *self-perceived* language proficiency is related to adjustment difficulties among international students (Wang, Lin, Pang, & Shen, 2006). Self-doubt (or doubts from other people) related to language issues may exacerbate anxiety, which in turn may negatively affect your actual performance (Wang, 2006). Therefore, it is critical that you focus your energy on improving your research and writing skills (e.g., being open to feedback, not taking criticism personally), rather than being defeated by feelings of inadequacy (e.g., "I can never write like a native English speaker!"; Wang, 2006). International students who experience language difficulties should seek out university resources such as writing centers to hone their English writing skills. Advisors should also provide international students with lots of encouragement and check their own assumptions in this process. It is important to recognize that not every international student experiences language barriers and that English proficiency does not equate to intellectual capacity.

Data Collection

It is essential to note any differences in research practice if you have already received some postbachelor training in psychology or have conducted research in your home country before coming to the United States. For example, in many countries, researchers are not required to have their research proposals approved by an independent institutional review board, yet this is a requirement for researchers in the United States. Students should check with their university's Human Subject Review Board and any other institutional review boards that are relevant to psychological research.

Students who aim to collect data from a specific population but are not enrolled in a university with access to a particular participant pool may consider the possibility of conducting Web-based surveys. Depending on the nature of your research question and design, it may be possible to collect data through electronic mailing lists, student organizations, and personal connections. It is important that you consult with your thesis or dissertation advisors and obtain approval from your committee before implementing a particular methodology.

Preparing for Prospectus and Defense Meetings

Presenting and defending a thesis or dissertation can be a stressful experience for international students who are anxious about orally describing and defending their research in a second language. It is advisable to practice your presentation before the actual defense. A well-designed presentation can benefit from visual aids such as a PowerPoint presentation. Visual aids help structure the presentation and provide details that may not need to be presented orally. Students are also encouraged, if not required by their program, to invite noncommittee members to attend the defense meeting because this can be good practice for later presenting their theses or dissertations for job interviews.

RESEARCH EXPERIENCES OUTSIDE THE THESIS OR DISSERTATION

All doctoral students are encouraged to engage in research activities outside the degree requirements of a thesis and dissertation because these experiences help improve students' research skills and can generate publications to build students' experience. It is particularly crucial that students who aspire to pursue an academic career obtain additional research experiences and accumulate publications to be a competitive candidate in the job market.

First- and 2nd-year students may begin to participate in research teams or assist faculty with their research grants. These experiences can help you build a knowledge base of information as well as develop good research skills. You may expand your research network through active involvement in professional organizations (e.g., APA or your state psychological association). Also, you may find opportunities for funding and data collection through collaborations with local agencies (e.g., industrial or organizational settings, community mental health agencies). These types of professional connections may be particularly important for students who are unable to find research mentors in their home institutions. In addition, you should consider your personal goals for participating in research projects (e.g., acquiring a specific skill) and consult with your advisor about your objectives and interests. It is easy to become overcommitted because of a desire to be involved in many exciting opportunities. You should make good decisions about the best use of your time.

More senior students should further develop their own research programs to establish themselves as experts in specific content areas. A research program focuses on a particular area of study with a number of research projects planned to systematically contribute new knowledge in that area. It establishes a psychologist as an expert in a specific field and is a critical task for any psychologist who is interested in an academic position within a research-oriented university. For psychologists who do not plan on academic careers, a good research background in graduate school will help practitioners understand and apply future research to their practice.

CONFERENCE PRESENTATIONS AND PUBLICATIONS

You should consider submitting your research for conference presentations and publications. You can gradually hone your writing skills by writing a more straightforward section of the manuscript first and then taking on other sections that require advanced skills and knowledge (Lin et al., 2006). For example, the methods and results sections may be easier to write than the discussion section because the former sections generally require straightforward descriptions of the participants, procedures, methods, and results. Once this skill has been mastered, you may practice writing more complex discussions of results, including implications for future theory and practice.

You are encouraged to submit research articles to top-tier peer-reviewed journals, including APA's journals, and adhere to the corresponding journal's submission guidelines. In addition, the *Publication Manual of the American Psychological Association, Fifth Edition* (APA, 2001) and *Presenting Your Findings: A Practical Guide for Creating Tables* and *Displaying Your Findings: A Practical Guide for Creating Figures, Posters, and Presentations* (Nicol & Pexman, 1999, 2003) provide detailed suggestions on how to prepare conference presentations and manuscripts for publication. Specifically, you are advised to (a) find a journal whose mission fits best with the manuscript; (b) follow the journal's exact submission instructions; (c) rely on trustworthy mentors and colleagues to read the drafts and advise them at every step; (d) remember that plagiarism is strictly prohibited (even the author's own work must be properly cited); and (e) learn from the reviews, revise and resubmit manuscripts in a timely fashion, and be persistent in the process of getting the research published.

The writing process provides the opportunity to learn how scholars negotiate publication credit. In an ideal situation, the order of authorship for presentations and manuscripts should be discussed at major stages of the research process. In the United States and within psychology, order of authorship is typically based on each individual's contribution to the study (Fine & Kurdek, 1993; Winston, 1985), although this may vary because of the purpose and goals of a particular project. In some countries (e.g., certain countries in Asia or the Middle East), authorship orders may be determined by seniority or status. Therefore, it might be difficult for some international students to assert first or higher-order authorship if their cultural values taught them to defer to senior authors. You should become familiar with the APA ethical guidelines on authorship and raise these issues with your research collaborators.

You are also encouraged to review conference proposals and manuscripts. Such experience provides you with opportunities to learn from cutting-edge research, refine your research evaluation skills, as well as articulate your analyses of the quality and potential contribution of a study. It is important to remember that you should only volunteer to review in your area of expertise. Furthermore, you should provide general recommendations and substantive critiques that manuscript authors can use to strengthen their studies. Reviews should be written in a professional manner that is respectful to the authors. Finally, you should be familiar with professional ethics related to the review process (e.g., confidentiality) and establish a reputation for turning in reviews on time, if not ahead of schedule.

FUNDING YOUR RESEARCH

You should investigate what type of research funding is available from your own institution by consulting with your advisor. Nonprofit organizations and for-profit corporations also offer various types of grants for research in areas that fit with their funding objectives, and some offer funding for a thesis or dissertation that relates to a specific topic or population, or that uses a particular methodology. More resources specific to research funding are listed in Appendix B.

Conclusion

In this chapter we discuss the fact that international students can obviously benefit from conducting research in the United States. Perhaps less obvious are the benefits that faculty and American students receive when they conduct research with international students. International students help facilitate the development of cross-cultural knowledge through their research endeavors and through their interactions with peers and faculty. The field of psychology also benefits from international students' research when new perspectives enlighten existing theories and practices. We hope that this chapter serves as a helpful guide in your journey and leads you to fruitful research, innovations, and international collaborations in psychology.

References

American Psychological Association. (2001). *Publication manual of the American Psychological Association* (5th ed.). Washington, DC: Author.

APA Presidential Task Force on Evidence-Based Practice in Psychology. (2006). Evidence-based practice in psychology. *American Psychologist, 61,* 271–285.

Fine, M. A., & Kurdek, L. A. (1993). Reflections on determining authorship credit and authorship order on faculty–student collaborations. *American Psychologist, 48,* 1141–1147.

Forum Qualitative Sozialforschung. (2007). *Online-Gateway for qualitative research.* Retrieved January 5, 2007, from http://www.qualitative-research.net/

Heppner, P. P., Casas, J. M., Carter, J., & Stone, G. L. (2000). The maturation of counseling psychology: Multifaceted perspectives, 1978–1998. In S. D. Brown & R. W. Lent (Eds.), *Handbook of counseling psychology* (3rd ed., pp. 3–49). New York: Wiley.

Heppner, P. P., & Heppner, M. J. (2004). *Writing and publishing your thesis, dissertation, and research: A guide for students in the helping professions.* Pacific Grove, CA: Brooks/Cole.

Lang, K. M. S. (2007). *Practical tips for completing your psychology dissertation: A recent graduate student's perspective.* Retrieved March 4, 2007, from http://www.apa.org/apags/edtrain/dissertationtips.html

Lin, Y.-J., Shen, F., & Wang, Y.-W. (2006, August). Tips on conducting research and writing your own thesis/dissertation. In Y.-W. Wang, Y.-J. Lin,

& P. Nyutu (Chairs), *International student orientation*. Roundtable discussions conducted at the 2006 annual meeting of the American Psychological Association, New Orleans, LA.

Nicol, A. A. M., & Pexman, P. M. (1999). *Presenting your findings: A practical guide for creating tables*. Washington, DC: American Psychological Association.

Nicol, A. A. M., & Pexman, P. M. (2003). *Displaying your findings: A practical guide for creating figures, posters, and presentations*. Washington, DC: American Psychological Association.

Ponterotto, J. G. (2005). Integrating qualitative research requirements into professional psychology training programs in North America: Rationale and curriculum model. *Qualitative Research in Psychology, 2*, 97–116.

Wang, Y.-W. (2006, August). *The training experiences of international students in Counseling Psychology*. Paper presented at the 2006 annual meeting of the American Psychological Association, New Orleans, LA.

Wang, Y.-W. (2008). Qualitative research. In P. P. Heppner, B. E. Wampold, & D. M. Kivlighan, Jr. (Eds.), *Research design in counseling* (3rd ed., pp. 256–295). New York: Brooks/Cole and Wadsworth.

Wang, Y.-W., Lin, J. G., Pang, L.-S., & Shen, F. C. (2006). International students from Asia. In F. Leong, A. G. Inman, A. Ebreo, L. Yang, L. M. Kinoshita, & M. Fu (Eds.), *Handbook of Asian American psychology* (2nd ed., pp. 245–261). Thousand Oaks, CA: Sage.

Winston, R. B. (1985). A suggested procedure for determining order of authorship in research publications. *Journal of Counseling and Development, 63*, 515–518.

INTERNSHIPS, POSTDOCS, AND EMPLOYMENT

VI

Ayşe Çiftçi and Carol Williams-Nickelson

Internships in Psychology: Special Considerations for International Students

12

The psychology predoctoral internship is a yearlong, full-time clinical training experience. It is a required part of the organized and sequential training needed to become a practicing psychologist. Internship occurs in the final year of a student's doctoral program, ideally after the student has defended, or at least proposed, his or her dissertation. Each fall, eligible students must submit a comprehensive application, travel to interviews at different training sites, and wait until February to learn whether they have been matched to an internship site. If a student is matched, her or his internship will begin the following academic year.

The internship application process is demanding and stressful for most applicants. The application process consists of recording clinical hours, creating curriculum vitae, articulating clear internship and career goals, interviewing at internship sites, and finally being matched to a site. An internship is one of the most valuable experiences that a graduate student will undertake as a budding practitioner (Williams-Nickelson & Keilin, 2005). However, the unique needs and requirements for international students may add additional stress to this process. Advance knowledge of and preparation for these considerations may ease the burden that some international students face. This chapter provides an overview of the general internship process and addresses the concerns that specifically pertain to international students who apply for internships.

A Review of the Internship Application Process

As an intern applicant, you are well advised to begin preparing for your internship at the beginning of your training program by strategically selecting particular types of practicum training and by carefully recording all training hours and clinical experiences. This type of planning and preparation may help all prospective interns identify the type of training still needed when they are ready to apply for internships.

ASSOCIATION OF PSYCHOLOGICAL POSTDOCTORAL AND INTERNSHIP CENTERS

The first step you need to take in preparing for an internship is to become familiar with the Association of Psychology Postdoctoral and Internship Centers (APPIC). You can learn about APPIC by searching the organization's Web site at http://www.appic.org. APPIC is an organization whose members are internship and postdoctoral training programs in the United States and Canada. APPIC oversees the internship selection process by providing resources such as the APPIC Application for Psychology Internship (AAPI), a directory of APPIC member internship sites, and services such as the APPIC Match and Clearinghouse. Although APPIC is not an accrediting agency, its members are required to meet certain criteria to be accepted for membership. Almost all of the internship sites accredited by the American Psychological Association (APA) and the Canadian Psychological Association are members of APPIC. For a current listing of APA-accredited internship programs, visit http://www.apa.org/ed/accreditation/.

Reviewing APPIC's online directory of internship sites and identifying those that fit well with your interests and training goals is an important activity early in the preparation process. In general, you should apply to 10 to 12 sites that are geographically diverse, with different levels of competitiveness (determined by the number of internship applicants compared with the number of positions available). A complete internship application packet must be submitted to each site and includes a cover letter, the AAPI, a curriculum vitae, recommendation letters, transcripts, and in some cases site specific materials, such as an additional essay question or work sample. It takes considerable time and thought to prepare a competitive application packet.

THE APPI AND OTHER APPLICATION MATERIALS

The AAPI is a uniform application that is a required part of the application packet for all APPIC member sites. This application is approximately

20 pages in length and will take several hours to complete, even with records of practicum hours, supervision hours, and other materials organized and on hand for reference. The AAPI may change from year to year; thus, it is important that you download the correct version for the year in which you are applying for an internship. The AAPI includes areas for you to record demographic information and clinical experiences such as psychotherapy, evaluation, testing, consultation, and supervision hours. It also poses five essay questions that are each limited to a 250-word response. Your training director must sign the AAPI to verify the information and indicate that you are ready for the type of training offered in the internship.

INTERVIEWS

In late fall, you will be notified about whether or not you have been selected for internship interviews. The number of interviews a student is invited to participate in may range from none to almost all depending on the qualifications of the candidate, the applicant pool, the quality of the candidate's application, and most important, the fit between the candidate and the internship site. Generally, however, students who have prepared well can usually expect to be invited to interview at about half the sites to which they applied. Interviews generally take place in December and January, and most are in person and require the candidate to travel at his or her own expense to the site. Other sites, such as those at many counseling centers, conduct only telephone interviews. Interviews range in format and style from standardized to free-flowing conversation. Some interviews may last from 30 minutes to 1 hour; other internship sites will schedule several interviews on the same day. A few sites give the option to choose a phone or on-site interview. Whenever possible, it is helpful to visit the site and meet with the staff. However, on-site interviews have financial implications for you. Deciding to accept an on-site or phone interview depends on your availability, ability to travel, and financial ability to pay for travel. Although it does not happen often, you may decline the offer for an interview if you are unable to afford the travel costs. In these cases, the site may offer a telephone interview. Most internship sites list whether they prefer and hold on-site or telephone interviews in the APPIC directory, along with information about their specific interview process. You can take this information into consideration when selecting the types of programs to which you will apply.

RANKING SITES AND THE APPIC MATCH

There are three main parts to the APPIC Match process. The first step is to register for the match with National Matching Services (NMS), a company specializing in professional matching services. This occurs in September or October. You may download registration forms for the Match from the NMS Web site at http://www.natmatch.com/psychint and mail them directly to NMS with the appropriate fee. You will then receive an e-mail confirmation of your registration with an applicant code number that uniquely identifies you for the purposes of the Match (Keilin, 2005).

The next step is for you to rank order the internship sites that you would like to attend. You should complete and submit your rank-ordered list in late January to early February. This is accomplished by determining the order of preference for the programs you would like to attend. There is no limit to the number of programs that you may rank, and all rankings from both students and programs remain confidential. According to Keilin (2005),

> The order in which you rank internship programs should reflect only your true preferences, without regard for how you think these programs have ranked you, whether the programs will be ranking you [at all], or what sort of pressure you might have experienced from others to rank programs. (pp. 94–95)

Similarly, internship sites will rank the students that they deem the best fit for their site in order of preference. The computer will then make the best match possible for both parties on the basis of an algorithm that has been specifically designed for this purpose. It is important that you do not rank any sites you would not want to attend if matched, as the results of the Match are binding on both parties.

The final step occurs in late February when you receive the Match results. Although there is a documented supply-and-demand problem that has grown each year since the inception of the Match, the majority of internship applicants are successfully matched through this program or clearinghouse (Keilin, Thorn, Rodolfa, Constantine, & Kaslow, 2000). Some of the main reasons students do not get placed through the Match system include geographical restrictions, applying to too few or too many competitive programs, unremarkable letters of recommendation, poorly written applications and essays, and the lack of a good and clear fit between an individual applicant, his or her training goals and needs, and the sites to which he or she applied. For those who do not match, the clearinghouse is a valuable resource that lists unfilled positions that are available after the Match. The APPIC Web site has extensive information on the operation of the clearinghouse. Many applicants report finding high-quality positions through the clearinghouse (Keilin, 2005).

Williams-Nickelson and Prinstein (2005) offer a comprehensive review of preparing for an internship from the beginning to the end of the process. They provide recommendations for completing the APPI, composing essays, writing application cover letters, interviewing, and participating in the Match. There are other resources for internship preparation, such as internship workshops at the annual APA convention, colloquia, and organized meetings on campuses. You need to remember that preparing for and applying to internship sites is a process that requires consistent effort and preparation over time. It is not something that can be done adequately in one sitting or the week prior to application deadlines. Overall, the key to obtaining a good internship training experience is finding the right fit between you and the internship site (Williams-Nickelson & Prinstein, 2005).

Special Issues for International Students Selecting Internship Sites

International students have to consider specific issues during the internship selection process such as legal restrictions, visa status, postgraduation plans and sites' openness to cross-cultural training.

INTERNATIONAL STUDENTS AND INTERNSHIP SITES

Each internship site has different requirements for the qualities and experiences they seek in prospective interns. These include a minimum number of clinical hours, certain types of clinical experiences, a student's training program (e.g., counseling, clinical), and nationality. For instance, unless there is a special circumstance such as a consortium arrangement, international students are ineligible to work at state or federal agencies such as Veteran's Administration (VA) hospitals, prisons, other correctional facilities, or in any branch of the U.S. military. For example, out of 605 APPIC member internship sites listed in the 2006–2007 APPIC online directory, 201 required U.S. citizenship (APPIC, 2006). Most of these 201 sites were VA medical centers ($n = 72$), followed by community mental health centers ($n = 17$), prisons or other correctional facilities ($n = 16$), state/county/other public hospitals ($n = 14$), consortiums ($n = 13$), armed forces medical centers ($n = 11$), and others such as medical schools, university counseling centers, and private general hospitals.

To find an appropriate fit, it is essential to fully research each site of interest. You should first determine whether U.S. citizenship is a requirement. If there are international students currently interning at the site, you may ask to talk with one of these interns about his or her experiences at the particular site. You may also want to evaluate how well the site includes multicultural issues in its mission statement and training opportunities, the diversity of the clientele, and overt support for postdoctoral training and job search opportunities. You can gather this information by talking with current interns, asking the training director, and asking pointed questions during the interview.

If you are one of the many international students who plan to remain in the United States, you should review state licensure requirements and eligibility criteria for any state in which you intend to practice. Some states will not grant licensure to non-U.S. citizens. The Association of State and Provincial Psychology Boards' Web site at http://www.asppb.org provides helpful information about licensure and certification. You should directly consult materials provided by your state licensing board for specific and up-to-date information.

PREPARATION TO RETURN HOME

Students planning to return to their home countries may want to develop their clinical skills at a site wherein cultural differences are especially appreciated and supported. As chapter 15 of this volume discusses, there are many issues a new psychologist faces when returning home. Preparing for this inevitable transition while training in the United States may help ease the stresses associated when these students return to their home countries armed with their new degrees and status as psychologists. As part of an ongoing project partially funded by a grant from the American Psychological Association of Graduate Students (APAGS) in 2006, the first author conducted qualitative research to explore international students' experience of competency as a final year trainee in psychology (Çiftçi, 2006). Interviews focused on supervision, evaluation, and interactions with clients, staff, and other interns. Interview questions also attempted to determine students' assessment of their readiness to enter the field. In these interviews, international interns expressed that they were able to provide therapy in their native language with clients from the same culture. The ability to deliver services to clients in a language that was different from the language of their supervisors was a possibility only after each intern and supervisor developed a trusting working relationship. However, this activity was critical to helping the international interns develop a competency that would be valuable when they returned home.

DIFFICULTY ACCESSING INFORMATION

International students may experience difficulty gathering information from their doctoral programs about internship requirements. The most common miscommunication between doctoral programs and international students stems from visa requirements and procedures. It is important that you have access to accurate and current information about visa requirements. Thus, you should not rely on faculty or programs to provide this information. Rather, you should communicate with your office of international affairs, if one exists on campus, and take personal responsibility for obtaining this information. If you are matched to an internship site that is in a different state than the one your university is in, you obviously must move. This move may result in visa concerns. More information about visas and work permits is available in chapter 6.

PREPARING FOR A TRANSITION

The internship application and training process has financial and emotional implications. As a prospective intern, you must register for the match and pay a fee for this service. There are also costs associated with mailing applications. However, the greatest expenses are usually related to travel. You are responsible for arranging and paying for your air, rail, or bus transportation to participate in interviews. Overnight stays are often necessary because of the length of the interview or the distance you have to travel, and you are responsible for these costs as well. Geographic restrictions or costs may affect the application and match process for students who do not have as much flexibility in these areas as their colleagues who are U.S. citizens. Relocation can be a challenge for many international interns. In Çiftçi's (2006) research, some international interns said that they avoided moving to a new place because they felt "ungrounded." In most cases, after having adjusted to living in the United States and becoming acclimated to the new culture, international interns prefer to avoid facing a similar transition for the yearlong internship. Some may also wish to continue accessing the social support they worked hard to build within their program.

VISA STATUS

You need to be aware of the regulations and changes that take place in regard to your visa. For F-1 visa students, a predoctoral internship may be considered optional practical training (OPT). OPT is a 12-month employment permit given to F-1 students on a temporary basis as an opportunity to apply knowledge from their education to practical work experience (U.S. Immigration and Customs Enforcement, 2006). A predoctoral internship is considered an OPT. However, if an international intern uses a predoctoral internship year as an OPT, she or he must leave the United States after the internship unless the student secures a job in which the employer will sponsor an H-1 visa. In some cases, depending on the site, postdoctoral training may be considered employment. If the intern is employed for any period less than 12 months, his or her predoctoral internship year is not considered an OPT. One way to facilitate this arrangement is by negotiating a contract of less than 52 weeks. This way, the intern can stay in the United States for 1 more year and use OPT for postdoctoral training or 1 year of employment. Although most sites have information about legal procedures for international interns, a student should advise his or her training director about his or her visa status and its requirements. To learn more about visa status and requirements, visit the U.S. Immigration and Customs Enforcement Web site at http://www.ice.gov/sevis/students/opt.htm.

When a student leaves his or her doctoral program for an internship, she or he usually must inform the home institute's international office. The home institution has the authority to decide how many weeks an intern may have in a contract, which will not count as OPT. Moreover, it is the responsibility of the student's home institution (usually an international office) to enter a student's information into the Student and Exchange Visitor Information System (SEVIS) system.[1] However, students are advised to check with their schools to ensure the completion of this requirement.

SUPERVISION AND RELATIONSHIPS WITH OTHERS AT THE INTERNSHIP SITE

Even though it takes time to develop a relationship with supervisors, you should be prepared to clearly communicate any special needs you may have. Informing a supervisor and other staff about your culture is critical to creating a comfortable environment based on mutual respect. If you are not a native English speaker you may have a more difficult time doing this. Language can also be a challenge for English-speaking internationals students such as Canadians and British. These students are often not seen as truly international, so their cultural differences may be ignored. It is important to be aware of cultural differences that extend beyond language, skin color, and physical appearance. For further discussion about language, please refer to chapter 3.

Although some interns report that they would prefer more discussion about cultural differences and how they affect their experiences in internships, others report that there are no opportunities for such discus-

---

[1]SEVIS is a system developed to keep updated and accurate information for students and visitors. It "enables schools and program sponsors to transmit mandatory information and event notifications via the Internet, to the Department of Homeland Security and Department of State throughout a student or exchange visitor's stay in the United States" (U.S. Department of State, 2007).

sions or that such conversations end by their being told to "adapt" to the culture. Finding ways to talk about cultural differences in an open manner with supervisors and others during an internship can create a more productive training environment. Asking for support from other international students or trusted faculty and staff is often helpful. Other resources for international graduate student interns are available through organizations such as APAGS (see http://www.apa.org/apags/listservs for more information). One of Çiftçi's (2006) project participants advises,

> Don't be ashamed of your culture, don't be ashamed of being different . . . I believe we need to promote these differences more. After all, it is a very rewarding and unique experience to bring our cultural differences to our work environment!

References

Association of Psychology Postdoctoral and Internship Centers. (2006, May 20). *2006 APPIC Match: Survey of internship applicants*. Retrieved January 20, 2007, from http://www.appic.org/match/5_2_2_4_8_match_about_statistics_surveys_2006.htm

Keilin, W. G. (2005). The Match. In C. Williams-Nickelson & M. J. Prinstein (Eds.), *Internships in psychology: The APAGS workbook for writing successful applications and finding the right match* (2005–2006 ed., pp. 93–100). Washington, DC: American Psychological Association.

Keilin, W. G., Thorn, E. E., Rodolfa, E. R., Constantine, M. G., & Kaslow, N. J. (2000). Examining the balance of internship supply and demand: 1999 Association of Psychology Postdoctoral and Internship Centers' Match implications. *Professional Psychology: Research and Practice, 31,* 288–294.

Çiftçi, A. C. (2006). [The competence level of international psychology interns]. Unpublished data.

U.S. Department of State. (2007, November). What is SEVIS and SEVP? What should you know about it? In *Student visas*. Retrieved December 5, 2007, from http://travel.state.gov/visa/temp/types/types_1268.html#sevis

U.S. Immigration and Customs Enforcement. (2006, November 20). *International students: Optional practical training*. Retrieved January 20, 2007, from http://www.ice.gov/sevis/students/opt.htm

Williams-Nickelson, C., & Keilin, W. G. (2005). Getting started: General overview of the internship application process. In C. Williams-Nickelson & M. J. Prinstein (Eds.), *Internships in psychology: The APAGS workbook for writ-*

ing successful applications and finding the right match (2005–2006 ed., pp. 3–10). Washington, DC: American Psychological Association.

Williams-Nickelson, C., & Prinstein, M. J. (2005). *Internships in psychology: The APAGS workbook for writing successful applications and finding the right match* (2005–2006 ed.). Washington, DC: American Psychological Association.

Shonali C. Raney, Bong Joo Hwang, and Louise A. Douce

Finding Postdoctoral Training and Employment in the United States

13

The experience of being an international student in the United States can be exciting, yet challenging. There are adjustments and considerations involved with a move to a new and unfamiliar country involving adaptation to a new culture, making new friends, and possibly learning a new language and academic system. Training does not end when you earn your degree. If you intend to practice psychology after receiving your doctoral degree and you become licensed to do so, most state licensure boards require formal postdoctoral training.

We designed this chapter as a guide to help you through the processes involved in applying for postdoctoral training, commonly referred to as a *postdoc*, after you have completed or are in the process of completing the predoctoral internship. We also discuss how to apply for full-time employment. Both processes involve similar tasks and we discuss issues that apply to both. Remember that postdoctoral positions are temporary and are meant to provide you with additional expertise before you secure a professional job.

Available Postdoctoral Positions

Postdoctoral training is required by most states as a licensing requirement. The goal of this training is to provide supervision and thereby beiter equip students to move on to professional practice or research. Postdoctoral training, therefore, is a stepping-stone for students to move from formal, supervised instruction to the professional realm. There are essentially three types of postdocs: research, clinical, and specialty training (e.g., neuropsychology). Research postdocs require trainees to work on specific research projects that are funded through grants. Clinical postdocs, however, primarily involve direct service and little or no research. A postdoctoral position may be Association of Psychology Postdoctoral and Internship Centers (APPIC)-approved or non-APPIC approved. APPIC is an organization whose members include agencies sponsoring pre- and postdoctoral training programs. Members must comply with APPIC's membership criteria and their programs are listed in a directory of for prospective interns.

These two different types of postdocs usually lead to different career paths. For example, research postdoctoral training prepares trainees for careers in research institutions that are affiliated with medical centers or universities, or for obtaining faculty positions at universities. Clinical positions help students obtain suitable employment at university counseling centers or community counseling centers and centers that address special issues such as addictions and eating disorders. You should investigate the different types of postdoctoral positions available each year and decide whether they fit your training needs and career goals. There are various ways to search for available postdoctoral positions. The most popular include searching the APPIC Online directory, subscribing to various listservs available through the American Psychological Association of Graduate Students and the American Psychological Association (APA), and reading through the positions advertised in *Monitor on Psychology*. We discuss specific job search procedures later in this chapter.

DETERMINING ELIGIBILITY

As you review different postdoctoral positions, you may find it helpful to gather and organize information about each site. For research positions, you need to know how much research is generated and whether this research is funded by grants. This information is necessary because research postdocs are often supported by these grants. Finding out that a site has a history of frequently being funded by grants gives you information about whether a position there is stable and whether that position might be renewed for longer than the 1-year contract. Some grants from institutions such as the National Institute of Mental Health specifically require first authors of grants to be U.S. citizens; therefore, you need to know whether or not you would be allowed to work at that site. This information can be obtained by asking the site supervisor or checking the site's Web site.

You need to read the job descriptions of clinical positions carefully to determine your eligibility, especially if the position involves working with specific populations. This process is similar to selecting an appropriate predoctoral internship. Many times the institution you are applying to might require your predoctoral training to be in the same area as the available position.

You also need to check whether the position requires a doctoral degree. The job description may state a doctoral degree is "required" or "desired." The latter requirement usually means that a candidate should have fulfilled all the requirements of a doctoral program and is working toward completion of his or her dissertation (i.e., All But Dissertation or ABD). A doctoral degree is therefore preferable, but not necessary, to secure the position. However, it is important to note that if you do not have the completed degree, you might be compared with other applicants who do.

JOB APPLICATION

If you have already gone through the predoctoral internship process, you may find the job application process for postdoc or senior staff positions is similar and in some cases, more intense. When you apply for jobs you will go through several steps, including: (a) searching for job announcements; (b) selecting positions to which you want to apply; (c) completing application materials and sending them out; (d) being selected for and going on interviews; and (e) getting job offers and negotiating terms of employment. The suggestions in the following sections are based on our experiences, which have been influenced by the book *Internships in Psychology: The APAGS Workbook for Writing Successful Applications and Finding the Right Match* (Williams-Nickelson & Prinstein, 2004), as two of us (Hwang and Raney) used the workbook when we went through the predoctoral internship application process.

Job Announcements

Finding available jobs has become a more complex process, as some jobs are advertised online on Web sites or announcements, some only in professional magazines, and some jobs are advertised using both outlets. You can obtain information about available jobs through Web sites (e.g., http://www.psychnet-uk.com/mental_health_jobs/psychology_specific.htm), professional magazines (e.g., *Monitor on Psychology*), and through electronic mailing lists or forwarded e-mail messages from your training director. You may find information about counseling center jobs from Positions in Counseling Centers, (see http://www2.kumc.edu/people/llong/picc/), but this list is not exhaustive. Some jobs may be announced only through professional magazines or through professional networks.

Selecting Positions

Choosing which positions to apply to can take a great deal of time and good organizational skills. We suggest that you select positions that you have a strong interest in and that are a good fit with your goals and interests. Good organizational skills will help you keep track of the jobs you are interested in and deadlines you must meet. When you first read about a job you are interested in, you should print a copy of the announcement to help keep information on various jobs separated and sorted. As you gather the copies of job announcements, you need to sort through them on the basis of the types of positions (e.g., research postdoc, clinical postdoc, specialty training), the degree of your interest (e.g., your interest level on a scale from 1–10), and the deadlines for application. You may also want to create a table to organize the information that you obtain. For example, you can create a table with sections for job description, deadline, contact information, required application materials, and your interest level.

Application Materials

A postdoctoral job application usually requires a cover letter, curriculum vitae, three to four recommendation letters, and official graduate transcripts. If you are applying for a research postdoc position you also have to provide a plan for a research project and perhaps a teaching plan, as a research position may also include a teaching responsibility. It is important to meet application deadlines, so allow enough time to work on gathering all required application materials. You also need to give enough time to your professional references to write the letters. You need to find someone who knows you well in terms of your personal and professional qualities and who can write a strong recommendation. We recommend you compose your cover letter in a way that allows the selection committee to get to know who you are without providing too many details about your personal life. You may want to ask a close friend, colleague, or family member whether the letter describes you well. In fact, it would be a good idea to ask someone who knows you well and has strong writing skills to read all the materials before you send them out.

Interviews

After you pass the initial screening based on your written application, you will be invited for an interview. Some sites conduct only phone interviews for postdoc positions, whereas others require the traditional two-step interview process, which includes phone and on-site interviews. The job announcement may provide you with information on the search process and the interview process. If it does not, you may want to contact the chair of the job search for additional information. The purpose of the interview is to allow the staff to obtain a better sense of who you are personally and professionally, and whether you fit with the job and the staff. It is also an opportunity for you to find out about the job and the people with whom you may end up working. We suggest you practice interviewing as much as you can to increase your chances of a successful interview. You need to organize all the materials you have gathered to answer interview questions and ask the interviewers about their site. If you are invited for an interview, the selection committee has decided that you have the ability to perform on the job; during the interview, committee members want to see whether you are able to connect with them on a personal level. Therefore, you need to be able to easily converse with other professionals about your personal, as well as professional, side.

If you are invited for an on-site interview after the initial phone interview, you are considered a top candidate for the job. The employer usually believes that anyone invited for an on-site interview is able to perform the tasks described on the job description. An on-site interview is likely to be very intensive. It consists of interviewing with many, if not all, staff members and giving one or two presentations. The presentations may be a case presentation and an outreach presentation for a clinical position. If you are invited to interview for a research postdoc position, you will have to present a research study that you have completed or will plan to do. Again, presenting yourself professionally and connecting with the staff are equally important to be considered a top candidate. Be prepared for the interviews and presentations by practicing, and then try to enjoy the interview process. When you are well prepared you may feel less anxious during the actual interview. A positive attitude, along with a sincere desire to learn about the job, will help you handle any anxiety and will also help you make a good impression.

Job Offers and Negotiation

Receiving a job offer is an exciting event, but it is not the end of the job search process. You should study the details of the job offer to see if you can negotiate the offer to meet your needs, such as fees for relocation, an increase in salary, or more vacation days. However, keep in mind that for a postdoctoral position there is unlikely to be a lot of room for negotiation. If the employer or job description does not say that the offer is non-negotiable, you can try to see if there is flexibility in the offer. After you get a written job offer, the offer cannot be dismissed until you decline it, so there is time for negotiation. If you have another job offer, you are in a better negotiating position. You will probably have a week or two to respond to the job offer. We did not find any empirical studies about the negotiation process of the postdoc position offer and are not aware of many anecdotes about it. You can at least ask if negotiation is possible. One author of this article (Hwang) asked an employer whether the offer was negotiable when he took a postdoc position, although the job offer did turn out to be non-negotiable.

Be Prepared for Rejection

You will probably receive more rejections than job offers or even invitations for interviews. It is hard to deal with any kind of rejection, but you need to be ready for it during a job search. First of all, you need to tell yourself that it is a necessary part of the whole process. Second, you have to remind yourself that it is not a rejection of you as a person. Third, it helps to remember that a rejection means that the site just found a better fit for the job. Fourth, you need to be optimistic that you will receive an offer that will be a better fit for you. When you do receive an offer, remember that there were other good applicants who were just not a good match for that position.

Overall, a job search is stressful and exciting at the same time. As you are likely to be involved in a busy work schedule (i.e., doing a predoctoral internship) as you begin your job search, good organization skills and sufficient time to prepare all necessary materials for application and interviews are needed. You may now realize the importance of having an individual with whom you can talk about your job search experiences. You will find that emotional support can help you get through the job search process. For example, one author of this article (Hwang) felt he was unqualified for many positions that he was applying to; however, talking about his feelings with his supervisor and receiving objective opinions about his qualifications was emotionally supportive. Therefore, having a mentor or someone who can relate to your experiences will be helpful; we recommend finding one.

TRANSITION TO POSTDOC

It is vital to know and communicate your visa status to your employer at the time of hire. You may be able to extend the student visa through your postdoc on the basis of the 2nd year as extended training required for licensure. If your postdoc is in another state, this may affect other areas, such as your driver's license. Knowing the specific laws of the state in which your academic program is located and the state in which you will be working during your postdoc is important. You may need to apply for an H-1B visa.

Employer Obligation for H-1B Visas

Employers do have specific obligations for supporting the H-1B visa. The position must be approved by U.S. Citizenship and Immigration Services (USCIS), which has regional offices. There are a number of steps you need to take in conjunction with the human relations office, including:

1. The position needs to be formally approved by the appropriate institution, must include a detailed job description, and the education (both degree status and major) or required experience must match your credentials.
2. The position job title must be submitted to the appropriate regional authority for "prevailing wage," which must be in line with the salary offered.
3. The position must be posted in at least two public places, announcing the position for domestic applicants. This is to justify hiring an international employee.
4. The letter to the USCIS needs to suggest "a uniquely qualified candidate" for the position and an indication that "no other candidate is more qualified for this position."

The employer pays a processing fee and often elects to pay for expedited review. The process can take several months and many employers will pay that fee to bring their new employees on board.

Again, candidates should be very clear about their current visa status and anticipated visa changes at the point of hire. Employers may have their own restrictions about timing in this process, depending on the employee policies of their institution. Employers should consult with an institutional expert for assistance in negotiating this process. Visas are granted by regional offices and judgments may not be consistent across the United States.

LICENSURE REQUIREMENTS FOR INTERNATIONALS

Currently, postdoctoral training opportunities do not require licensure in the jurisdiction of their location. Many postdoctoral residencies and fellowships were established to provide the year of postdoctoral supervision required for eligibility for licensure in most jurisdictions. After the APA changed the Model Licensing procedures in 2005, several states are starting to move eligibility for licensure at the point of degree. It is not clear how this will affect postdoctoral training.

We believe the field will evolve over the next decade. It is possible that some postdoctoral specialty training (e.g., prescriptive authority) may require licensure as well as completion of degree before admission to the program.

Moving and Settling in During the Postdoc

Before moving to a new city, you can ask your employer to help you obtain information about housing and transportation. Among other relocation concerns, you should ask about areas that have good school systems if you have children. Most postdoctoral positions do not compensate you for moving costs, so you should factor those costs into your budget. Remember that every state has its own laws and regulations about obtaining a driver's license. In Ohio, for example, you need to take your passport, I-20, and the optional practical training (OPT) card when applying for a license, and this license is only valid until the end of the OPT.

Funding, Salary, and Benefits

As an international postdoc, you need to consider whether the position is fully funded, how many months or years it is funded, and whether the position might be renewed. Of course, you need to know the salary and whether it is acceptable. Finally, you need to know what benefits are funded by the institution and whether they cover your particular needs (e.g., health insurance, dental and vision insurance plans, retirement funds). You should also find out whether benefits change with the type of funding.

Work-Related Issues

When you accept a position you need to know the time period of the postdoctoral training. Some appointments are for a period of 9 months, although others are for 12 months, with the possibility of renewal for an additional period of time.

Practical Issues

Are reasonably priced accommodations in the city or town of the postdoc available? If you have children, you need to know whether childcare facilities are available and whether you need to be on a waitlist for care.

Reference

Williams-Nickelson, C., & Prinstein, M. J. (2004). *Internships in psychology: The APAGS workbook for writing successful applications and finding the right match* (2004–2005 ed.). Washington, DC: American Psychological Association.

INTERNATIONAL STUDENTS: TRANSITIONING TO PSYCHOLOGISTS

Nadia T. Hasan, Nadya A. Fouad, and Raymond D. Fowler

International Students and Professional Development

14

I n this chapter we define professional development and discuss issues related to the professional development of international graduate students studying psychology in the United States. We also discuss recommendations for enhancing the professional development of these students, and we provide specific recommendations to help international students identify potential opportunities to foster professional development. We also provide recommendations for advisors who wish to assist international graduate students in their professional development journey.

Professional development is an important component of the training experience for psychology graduate students (Dodgen, Fowler, & Williams-Nickelson, 2003; Ducheny, Alletzhauser, Crandell, & Schneider, 1997; Gustitus, Golden, & Hazler, 1986; Spruill & Benshoff, 2001). Professional development has been known by various terms, including *professional identity, professional socialization, postgraduate development, developmental stages,* and *professionalism* (Ducheny et al., 1997). Professional development is a process that begins during graduate training and continues throughout an individual's development as a psychologist (Dodgen et al., 2003; Ducheny et al., 1997; Gustitus et al., 1986; Spruill & Benshoff, 2001). This chapter focuses on the early aspects of professional development that occur during graduate school.

Although professional development is considered a key aspect of training, it has been defined differently by various researchers. For the purposes of this discussion, professional development is defined as "an ongoing process through which an individual derives a cohesive sense of professional identity by integrating the broad-based knowledge, skills, and attitudes within psychology with one's values and interests" (Ducheny et al., 1997, p. 89). According to this definition, it is important for graduate students to integrate what they have learned in their academics with their values and interests. It is equally important for graduate students to be able to articulate what their professional identity means to them at different developmental stages, identify their professional development needs and evaluate whether they are being met, and monitor this throughout their educational experience (Ducheny et al., 1997). Some values and interests of international students may be different from those of domestic students, and as such, the professional development of international students has unique characteristics and is the focus of this chapter.

International Students and Professional Development

Professional development is essential for all graduate students in psychology and especially for international students who study psychology in the United States. Although research suggests that the majority of international students report feeling satisfied with their overall educational experience in the United States, most international students face academic, cultural, social, financial, and psychological challenges (Gulgoz, 2001; Sam, 2001; Yeh & Inose, 2003). Specific concerns for international students include homesickness, grades, anxiety, depression, time management, English language competence, and relationship management (Gulgoz, 2001; Yi, Lin, & Kishimoto, 2003).

International students' additional adjustments and challenges may come from four sources: culture shock, the ambassador role, adolescent emancipation, and academic stresses (Lin, 2000; Sam, 2001). Culture shock involves the problems encountered in dealing with life in a new cultural setting, such as negotiating daily social activities. The ambassador role occurs when international students are made to feel as an informal cultural representative of their country. Adolescent emancipation relates to establishing oneself as an independent, self-supporting, and responsible member of society. Academic stresses are the stresses associated with higher education, such as taking exams and completing papers. Although the latter two areas of adjustment are common to all graduate students, international students face specific academic stressors that are related to their status. These specific stressors include understanding a different grading system, selecting courses, learning relevant study skills, feeling competent when reading, writing, and speaking in English, understanding lectures, understanding the different expectations of different instructors, understanding and accepting the competitiveness of classmates, learning to synthesize and draw conclusions from the material, and understanding American policies regarding plagiarism (Gulgoz, 2001; Lin, 2000; Sam, 2001).

Despite the various forms of adjustment, concerns, and problem sources that international students experience, most report an overall satisfying experience with their training (Lin, 2000; Sam, 2001). International students who were satisfied were those who reported having good language skills, more social support, more contacts with U.S. students, many friends, satisfaction with finances, and being given information prior to coming to the United States (Lin, 2000; Sam, 2001). The professional development recommendations that follow were identified from the experiences of international graduate students reported in the literature, the literature on professional development, and the personal experiences of the authors. By following the recommendations for professional development provided in this chapter, you can increase your chances of being satisfied with your training experience and can maximize your career advancement, whether you return home or remain in the United States for further work or training.

PROFESSIONAL DEVELOPMENT: RECOMMENDATIONS FOR INTERNATIONAL GRADUATE STUDENTS

1. You are encouraged to create and maintain a shadow curriculum that relates to your interests and future career plans. A shadow curriculum consists of additional readings that are not part of the program curriculum. The additional readings are selected, monitored, and maintained by you. This can be a wonderful way to enhance the learning experience by helping establish expertise in a specific area of interest. The shadow curriculum can lead to additional opportunities to present at conferences, and it demonstrates initiative. Keeping up with the program curriculum is important, but maintaining a shadow curriculum will help you stand out in your cohort. Faculty advisors may help to identify the readings for a shadow curriculum.

2. You may want to engage in additional research projects, supplemental practicum experiences, or taking on leadership roles within organizations that relate to your interests and future career goals. The U.S. educational system is competitive and completing extra projects will help you enhance your skills and advance in your career.

3. You should consider establishing and maintaining a professional Web site that details your professional qualifications. Electronic

information is easy to find and it serves as an effective means of communication. Web sites are inexpensive and they are a useful way to inform faculty, other students, and potential employers about your qualifications. Put the Web site address on a university name card and distribute it widely.

4. You are encouraged to update your professional curriculum vitae often and use it as an evaluation tool to assess your progress each semester. You are encouraged to set up appointments with your advisor to review it and receive feedback about your work. Having an updated curriculum vitae is essential because most application processes request one.

5. You might benefit from seeking out opportunities to present your research in poster presentations, symposia, roundtables, and workshops. Several psychology organizations provide specific opportunities for graduate students to submit their work (Dodgen et al., 2003; Spruill & Benshoff, 2001). Poster presentations are often reserved for graduate student presenters. Presenting research is an excellent way to build curriculum vitae, meet colleagues, and make your work visible to the psychological community. Try to make at least one presentation each year of graduate training.

6. You may want to learn about and practice the art of networking. Networking is about building trust and working relationships with psychologists, other students, and potential employers (Speisman, 2006). It is important to be genuine and authentic when talking with other individuals. It is also advisable to clarify your goals for participating in a networking experience. Conferences and workshops provide excellent opportunities to network.

7. You should identify appropriate mentors by joining informal and formal mentoring programs to help connect and learn from psychologists or advanced graduate students during training. Many professional organizations, such as the American Psychological Association of Graduate Students (APAGS) and some state psychological associations, offer mentoring programs (Dodgen et al., 2003). It is important for you to connect with other psychologists who were international students or who have had experience working with them. These individuals will be helpful in advancing your growth and providing relevant information about navigating the U.S. educational system.

8. You may want to reach out to other graduate students, especially other international students, and create formal or informal support groups to provide personal and academic support as you advance in your graduate training. These students can be members of the same program or graduate students from different programs. Using Listservs and other electronic forms of commu-

nication make connecting with other individuals easy and inexpensive. For instance, APAGS provides a free listserv for international graduate students to discuss issues related to their training experiences. To join this listserv visit the APAGS homepage and access the listserv link.

9. Seek out leadership opportunities by volunteering to be a student representative in a psychology organization, state psychological association, or department, college, or university. Be proactive when seeking leadership positions and ask about adding student representatives to committees or organizations that you are interested in joining. If selected to serve, be consultative with fellow students to better represent their views.

10. You may want to join professional organizations at the program, local, state, regional, national, and international levels (Dodgen et al., 2003; Gustitus et al., 1986; Spruill & Benshoff, 2001). There are many benefits to joining psychology organizations, such as networking, feeling connected to the discipline, obtaining access to Listservs and Web sites, becoming eligible for awards and scholarships, leadership opportunities, opportunities to present work at conferences, reduced conference registration fees, and discounts on journals and other products. Organizations often provide reduced membership fees for graduate students; some offer a specific membership category for international members. To learn more about getting involved in professional organizations, see "Getting Involved in Professional Organizations: A Gateway to Career Advancement" by Dodgen, Fowler, and Williams-Nickelson (2003).

INTERNATIONAL STUDENTS AND PROFESSIONAL DEVELOPMENT: RECOMMENDATIONS FOR ADVISORS

The professional development of graduate students is the responsibility of all professionals and professional organizations (Spruill & Benshoff, 2001). Advisors play a valuable role in the professional development of international students (Gulgoz, 2001). International students not only face the academic issues associated with graduate education but they also face additional issues related to adjusting to a new country. Therefore, it is important for advisors to assist international students in their professional development and help them successfully transform themselves into psychologists (Gulgoz, 2001; Spruill & Benshoff, 2001). The recommendations that follow are based on the literature and the personal experiences of the authors. By following these recommendations, it is hoped that advisors who work with international students will feel empowered to assist the students with their professional development needs. Please see chapter 9 for additional information about relationships between international graduate students and advisors.

1. Advisors are encouraged to learn about the international student's country of origin, especially its cultural traditions, and discuss how the student is adjusting to life in the United States.
2. Advisors are encouraged to talk about the importance of being culturally centered and discuss how to handle cultural misunderstandings that might occur in the student–advisor relationship.
3. Advisors can informally share their own doubts, issues, dilemmas, attitudes, and values with international students to reduce students' feelings of isolation (Spruill & Benshoff, 2001).
4. Advisors are encouraged to invite international students to attend and present workshops with them at professional conferences. Advisors may also encourage students to submit proposals for state, regional, and national conferences. This will help students integrate and synthesize classroom learning, increase their confidence, develop expertise in a topic area, and network with other professionals (Spruill & Benshoff, 2001).
5. Invite students to be involved in research projects, manuscript writing, manuscript submission, and other aspects of the publication process, and give them credit for their contributions (Spruill & Benshoff, 2001). This will give international students the opportunity to work with faculty and develop strong relationships that can turn into mentoring and networking opportunities.
6. Recruit international students to serve as representatives on departmental boards, committees, and other leadership positions in college or university settings (Spruill & Benshoff, 2001). Students can bring enthusiasm and energy to meetings as well as provide a fresh perspective.
7. Promote participation in professional organizations and assist students in networking and connecting with other psychologists in their areas of interest. Advisors can also help students obtain research funding and opportunities, time off to attend professional meetings, and obtain the funding to attend conferences.
8. Most important, advisors can model professionalism for international students so they have an example of how a professional psychologist behaves (Spruill & Benshoff, 2001).

Conclusion

Life as a graduate student in another country can be an exciting and rewarding educational and cultural experience. In general, international graduate students are confronted with more challenges than domestic students, but there are ways to overcome these challenges. By working hard and taking on extra assignments and projects, academic anxieties can be overcome as students build personal competencies. Reaching out to others and building a social network can minimize feelings of loneliness, homesickness, and isolation. Establishing and nurturing a mentor relationship with a faculty member or more advanced student helps an international student adapt to the academic and social environment and profit from the wisdom of more experienced psychologists. We list some useful techniques drawn from the literature and our own experiences and these may be helpful. But it is important for you, the international student, to realize that most of the factors that ensure a successful and satisfying educational experience are in your own hands; it is the students who take the initiative, focus on the critical variables, and maintain an optimistic attitude who are the most likely to succeed.

References

Dodgen, D., Fowler, R., & Williams-Nickelson, C. (2003). Getting involved in professional organizations: A gateway to career advancement. In M. Prinstein & M. Patterson (Eds.), *The portable mentor: Expert guide to a successful career in psychology* (pp. 221–233). New York: Kluwer Academic/ Plenum Publishers.

Ducheny, K., Alletzhauser, H., Crandell, D., & Schneider, T. (1997). Graduate student professional development. *Professional Psychology: Research and Practice, 28,* 87–91.

Gulgoz, S. (2001). Stresses and strategies for international students. In S. Walfish & A. K. Hess (Eds.), *Succeeding in graduate school: The career guide for psychology students* (pp. 159–170). Mahwah, NJ: Erlbaum.

Gustitus, C., Golden, J., & Hazler, R. (1986). Graduate student development: An extracurricular approach. *Journal of Counseling and Development, 64,* 461.

Lin, J.-C. G. (2000). College counseling and international students. In D. C. Davis & K. M. Humphrey (Eds.), *College counseling: Issues and strategies for a new millennium* (pp. 169–183). Alexandria, VA: American Counseling Association.

Sam, D. L. (2001). Satisfaction with life among international students: An exploratory study. *Social Indicators Research, 53,* 315–337.

Speisman, S. (2006). *Ten tips for successful business networking.* Retrieved January 8, 2007, from http://www.businessknowhow.com/tips/networking.htm

Spruill, D. A., & Benshoff, J. M. (2001). The future is now: Promoting professionalism among counselors-in-training. *Journal of Counseling and Development, 74,* 468–471.

Yeh, C. J., & Inose, M. (2003). International students' reported English fluency, social support satisfaction, and social connectedness as predictors of acculturative stress. *Counselling Psychology Quarterly, 16,* 15–28.

Yi, J. K., Lin, J.-C. G., & Kishimoto, Y. (2003). Utilization of counseling services by international students. *Journal of Instructional Psychology, 30,* 333–342.

Amanda C. Kracen, Pia Zeinoun, J. Juana Wu, and Michael J. Stevens

Home Sweet Home: Issues for International Students to Consider When Returning Home

15

S tudying abroad is a unique experience for which most students adequately prepare; however, returning home after completion of studies is a momentous experience that often receives less preparation. International students can benefit from considering the issues involved in this major transition before the journey home. Therefore, in this chapter we review reasons international students return home, the adjustment process, challenges and benefits of returning home, the use of education and training gained in the host country, and job hunting. Additionally, we offer recommendations on how you can minimize potential adjustment challenges and provide strategies to help you find employment in your home country.

Reasons for Returning Home

Almost all international students ask themselves whether they will return home after completing their academic programs. Some decide to stay and work in the United States after finishing their studies. Many others decide to return to their home countries. The decision process is very personal and complex in nature. International students often feel pushed and pulled by people and opportunities from both their host and home countries.

Some international students volunteer to return home for many reasons. First, globalization has increased career opportunities all over the world. Thus, a degree from an American university and the additional experience abroad often provide career and economic advantages in the home country. In contrast, international students often perceive greater competition, more stress, and even prejudice or discrimination when seeking employment opportunities in the United States (Frey & Roysircar, 2006).

Second, cultural identity is another factor international students consider when they choose to return home. They may have a greater commitment to their home culture and experience a lack of belonging in American society because of differences in language, values, social practices, or holiday celebrations, to name a few. International students may feel marginalized in the host country as a result of their minority membership (Schmitt, Spears, & Branscombe, 2003).

Third, relationships with family and friends are common motivators to return home. Most international students have left family and friends to pursue their studies. Despite the friendships and social network established in the United States, many students want to be reunited with their family and friends at home (Arthur, 2004). They may feel obligated to return home to undertake family responsibilities, such as taking care of elderly family members. Finally, international students may decide to return home because of patriotism or a sense of responsibility to serve and contribute to their home countries. Thus, they may decide to return home in spite of their preference for life in the United States.

Although some international students return home by choice, others return involuntarily. Students may have to leave the United States and return home because of a failure to maintain good academic standing or to conform to immigration regulations. Depending on their visas, some students are mandated to complete a residency requirement in their home country after completing their education in the United States. Those who have received financial support from their home countries are often obligated, as a condition of the funding, to return. There are also specific reasons students may have to leave the host country. For example, students from Israel and Korea may have to return home to fulfill military service requirements (Light, 2002). Similarly, contractual obligations to fill a previously held job or otherwise serve the home country (e.g., mandatory social service) can necessitate students' return home. You are encouraged to contact your individual embassy and your university's international studies office to investigate country-specific policies and requirements.

READJUSTMENT TO HOME

You can benefit by anticipating reacculturation and reentry issues, which constitute challenges in readjusting to the home culture. Reacculturation and reentry is a process of transition into your culture of origin after having lived or worked overseas for an extended period (Martin, 1984). Although readjustment is expected, it is not necessarily a universal or problematic process (Brabant, Palmer, & Gramling, 1990; Tsang-Feign, 1993). Variables that affect readjustment to home culture include gender, age, number of sojourns abroad, the location and duration of the sojourn, and readiness to reenter (Brabant et al., 1990; Martin, 1984). More women than men report problems with family, friends, and daily life, suggesting that women may change more than men while away. Younger returnees report more readjustment problems, perhaps because they have less established personal identities and work roles. Repeated sojourns abroad ease readjustment because of familiarity with the process and a preparedness to cope with reentry. International students who spend considerable time in an unfamiliar host culture may experience more reacculturation challenges, as they are likely to have absorbed alternative worldviews and customs. Returnees who wish to remain overseas tend to resist reacculturation and may have less positive reentry outcomes.

International students' readjustment to their home cultures is conceptualized as a stage sequence, although the process is fluid (International Student Exchange Program, 2005; Martin, 1984; Tsang-Feign, 1993). Disengagement begins while the student is overseas and entails seeking closure on the sojourn and preparing for reentry. Euphoria characterizes the immediate prospect of reentry and the "honeymoon" shortly thereafter. Alienation follows as daily life resumes, with feelings of disorientation, loneliness, and helplessness. Gradual readjustment involves steady reacculturation, ideally through active integration of sojourn experiences into life at home.

Successful readjustment begins while international students are still abroad and continues after reentering their home cultures (Citron & Mendelson, 2005). You may find it helpful to maintain contact with family and friends electronically and, if possible, through a visit. You can stay up-to-date on the lives of family and friends and events in general. Before returning, you should identify reentry challenges that may apply and recognize that they are normative and require time to resolve. You will benefit from reflecting on personal changes and how to integrate these into life at home. You can gain closure by informing friends in the host culture how you have been affected by your friendships and by gathering memorabilia and contact information. After reentry, you should monitor your reactions to being home and situate them in the larger context of readjustment. You will benefit from sharing experiences and readjustment difficulties selectively with family, friends, and others who have traveled or lived abroad. You can gradually integrate the knowledge and skills acquired overseas into everyday life, thereby growing personally and professionally long after reentry.

Resources available to facilitate successful readjustment include books (e.g., *Self-Help for Foreigners: How to Keep Your Life, Family and Career Intact While Living Abroad*), journals (e.g., *International Journal of Intercultural Relations*), organizations whose Web sites offer handbooks (e.g., International Student Exchange Program at http://www.isep.org and Academy for Educational Development at http://www.aed.org), online magazines (e.g., *Transitions Abroad* at http://www.transitionsabroad.com), and university Web sites (e.g., http://www.internationalstudies.ilstu.edu/studentserve/StudentReturn.shtml), although relatively few university sites provide information for international students.

CHALLENGES AND BENEFITS OF RETURNING HOME

As already discussed, returning home after studying abroad is a major transition that has both challenges and benefits. Potential challenges following reentry include difficulty explaining your experiences and their effects, lack of interest by others in your experiences, inability to apply knowledge and skills acquired abroad, changes in relationships with family and friends, and criticism for adopting foreign attitudes and behaviors (International Student Exchange Program, 2005). Some students struggle with a tendency to compare host and home countries, feelings of frustration regarding their home society, and changes in the freedoms they have (Christofi & Thompson, 2007; Thompson & Christofi, 2006). You can face additional challenges, including differences in how advanced and cohesive the field of psychology is in your home country, availability of resources (e.g., equipment, journals, supervisors), recognition of graduate studies and graduate degrees by people in the home country, and opportunities for employment. Negative reactions following reentry can include emotional lability (e.g., anger, depression, elation), boredom after a stimulating sojourn, homesickness for the host culture along with disappointment and discomfort with your home culture, and fear of forgetting overseas experiences.

On arriving home, most international students enjoy returning to family, friends, and national culture. Many recognize that a greater self-awareness and internal growth has occurred as a result of their unique experiences (Christofi & Thompson, 2007). They are often excited to use what they have learned in their graduate studies and may be eager to share techniques and technologies with people in their home country. Additionally, they may be highly respected for having studied abroad and completed a graduate degree. Positive reactions on reentry can include confidence in one's adaptability, tolerance for ambiguity, ability to communicate, appreciation of diversity, and sense of global connectedness and responsibility (Citron & Mendelson, 2005).

USE OF EDUCATION AND TRAINING AT HOME

Graduate students return home to use their education and training; unfortunately, the small body of research on returnees focuses little attention on the challenges they face in applying new skills and knowledge in their home country (Mitchell, 2006). There are a variety of issues to consider, including adapting and communicating your education and training, being cautious in applying Western approaches, and sharing personal experiences.

Students frequently perceive a discrepancy between the high level of competency they have attained and the status quo of education, training, and market needs in their home countries. Young professionals can struggle to apply their new skills in their society and consequently may feel frustrated (Woody, 1998) and perhaps even isolated. To combat discouragement, you should consider how your skills can be used in your home country and be able to communicate unique credentials to colleagues and potential employers. In addition to considering how your skills can be used in traditional ways, you might also look into creating new positions based on your academic and professional background.

You should be cautious when applying the knowledge and skills you acquired studying abroad. Psychological science and practice as constituted in the United States should not be used indiscriminately. Early career professionals may be eager to share innovative theories and interventions with their home country. Although well-intentioned, there are risks to applying psychological interventions without cultural considerations.

Many international students find that psychological training and education achieves its full potential when disseminated to other individuals and to society. During training, you may acquire skills that are scarce, yet needed, in your home county. After studying abroad, you are in a position to disseminate your knowledge and skills with colleagues through conferences, workshops, and training sessions; in turn, these individuals can perpetuate the dissemination process. Personal resources can also be shared with current students (who are the rising cohort of psychologists) through workshops, lectures, and guest appearances in classes. As a returning graduate, you can be an agent of social change by using your skills for community growth and for enriching the individual. You can collaborate with local organizations to use your training to serve the interests of the community and society. Additionally, at a societal level, you can share your knowledge and skills through media interviews (see http://www.apa.org/journals/media/homepage.html).

A final opportunity returning students have is the chance to serve as a cross-cultural mediator. By being a global public relations officer, you can facilitate collaboration between researchers and practitioners in the United States and colleagues at home. Moreover, you can share your knowledge of how society and in particular the educational system operate in the sojourn country. You may also help students and scholars who are considering training abroad or are seeking resources (e.g., contacts, literature, organizations). You can inform colleagues of the opportunities and resources available and the various means to obtain and use them.

STRATEGIES TO FIND A JOB AT HOME

Finding a job can be challenging and anxiety provoking, especially after the investment of earning a graduate degree abroad. At the outset, the process may be overwhelming. However, there are numerous strategies that can help lessen your worries and increase your likelihood of securing a job. The following recommendations are intended to help international students, but the applicability of each depends on the particular home country. You are encouraged to adapt these tips to suit your individual situation.

1. *Commence the job hunt before going home.* As the process of finding a job varies greatly in length, it is best to start looking as soon as possible, even a few years in advance. Early preparation gives you time to explore options, ensure your training will be adequate for working in your home country, and develop contacts with potential employers.

2. *Visit the career center.* Colleges and universities frequently have a career center, although the extent to which they provide useful services to international students differs (Shen & Herr, 2004). However, you may benefit from exploring the services that are available and requesting help from staff.

3. *Research the qualifications required to work in your home country.* Requirements, accreditation, and licensure issues vary by country. Therefore, you need to be aware of these requirements to satisfy them and seek jobs that are consistent with your training. You may find it helpful to contact your country's national psychology association, if one exists (see http://www.apa.org/international/resources.html).

4. *Assess the job market in your country.* You will benefit by being aware of economic trends, opportunities for psychologists, and settings in which psychologists are typically employed.

5. *Consider the type of job desired.* As the field of psychology might differ greatly or not even exist in the home country, you may benefit by exploring both traditional and nontraditional employment options. There may be exciting, satisfying ways to use psychology graduate training in unique settings (e.g., businesses, military, nonprofit organizations).

6. *Seek a mentor.* A person "in the know" can be invaluable, especially someone in the field who can provide advice, guidance, and support. When selecting a mentor, you might consider former teachers and leaders in the field. Additionally, you may find it helpful to contact the country's national psychology association (see http://www.apa.org/international/resources.html) or other specialty organizations and ask for recommendations for possible mentors.

7. *Consider culture-specific issues.* You may have issues to think about that are country-specific. For instance, students returning to Cyprus have identified *meson*, or the social connections required to get a job, as a critical factor in finding employment at home (Thompson & Christofi, 2006). You will benefit by discussing these issues with mentors and others who are well acquainted with your home country.

8. *Reflect on personal strengths.* It is important to recognize that studying abroad is a rich experience that can be marketed to potential employers. International students often have distinctive attributes, such as a global educational experience, unique psychological training, multicultural experiences, and the ability to speak another language. These strengths can be highlighted when you are applying for jobs.

9. *Develop a curriculum vitae (CV) or similar document.* You should tailor your CV to the norms and standards of your home country. Additionally, it may help to provide explanations for aspects that may differ or not be understood. For instance, if a potential employer is unfamiliar with specific terminology, you may need to explain a training experience in detail. You will benefit from asking mentors and colleagues to review your CV to ensure it is clear and culturally appropriate.

10. *Network!* You should take the initiative to seek out potential employers and other people who can assist you in finding a job. It is frequently helpful to talk with mentors, professors, colleagues, conference attendees, members of professional organizations, and members of electronic mailing lists. It also helps to let people in both countries know about an active job search. Additionally, networking takes many forms, including meetings, phone calls, and e-mails. Visits home can be ideal occasions to pursue networking opportunities.

11. *Become a member of the home country's national psychology association.* Getting involved in professional organizations helps students meet people in the field and keep abreast of opportunities in the psy-

chological community. You can learn about jobs by reading newsletters and journals, joining electronic mailing lists, and the like.

12. *Pursue standard approaches.* You should not neglect typical strategies used to find jobs. You might find your dream job by scouring newspaper classified ads, searching Web sites for international jobs, or reading the American Psychological Association's *Monitor on Psychology*. You may also cold call a potential employer to ask about job opportunities, which can be done by e-mailing, telephoning, or writing a letter.

As with other major life transitions, returning home after graduate study in another country is a mixed blessing. International students typically experience a range of thoughts and emotions, both positive and negative. However, all too frequently students do not acknowledge or explicitly examine the issues involved in this transition. The issues raised and recommendations provided in this chapter are intended to help you make the process more intentional, thereby enhancing your study abroad experience and the reacculturation process.

References

Arthur, N. (2004). Re-entry transition: The transition from host to home cultures. In A. J. Marsella (Series Ed.) & N. Arthur (Vol. Ed.), *International and cultural psychology: Vol. 2. Counseling international students: Clients from around the world* (pp. 51–63). New York: Kluwer Academic/Plenum Publishers.

Brabant, S., Palmer, C. E., & Gramling, R. (1990). Returning home: An empirical investigation of cross-cultural reentry. *International Journal of Intercultural Relations, 14,* 387–404.

Christofi, V., & Thompson, C. L. (2007). You cannot go home again: A phenomenological investigation of returning to the sojourn country after studying abroad. *Journal of Counseling and Development, 85,* 53–63.

Citron, J., & Mendelson, V. (2005, July/August). *Coming home: Relationships, roots, and unpacking.* Retrieved March 1, 2007, from http://www.transitionsabroad.com/publications/magazine/0507/coming_home_from_study_abroad.shtml

Frey, L. L., & Roysircar, G. (2006). South Asian and East Asian international students' perceived prejudice, acculturation, and frequency of help resource utilization. *Journal of Multicultural Counseling and Development, 34,* 208–222.

International Student Exchange Program. (2005). *Participant handbook.* Retrieved March 1, 2007, from http://www.isep.org/students/placed/student_handbook.asp

Light, J. (2002, February 15). International students return home to serve country. *The Yale Herald, 33*(5). Retrieved March 8, 2007, from http://www.yaleherald.com/article. php?Article=244

Martin, J. N. (1984). The intercultural reentry: Conceptualization and directions for future research. *International Journal of Intercultural Relations, 8,* 115–134.

Mitchell, P. (2006). Revising effective reentry programs for returnees from U.S. academic programs. *Institutional and Development Group occasional papers.* Retrieved March 7, 2007, from http://www.aed.org/ToolsandPublications/upload/Re-Entry%20Paper%20(Final).pdf

Schmitt, M. T., Spears, R., & Branscombe, N. R. (2003). Constructing a minority group identity out of shared rejection: The case of international students. *European Journal of Social Psychology, 33,* 1–12.

Shen, Y.-J., & Herr, E. L. (2004). Career placement concerns of international graduate students: A qualitative study. *Journal of Career Development, 31,* 15–29.

Thompson, C. L., & Christofi, V. (2006). Can you go home again? A phenomenological investigation of Cypriot students returning home after studying abroad. *International Journal for the Advancement of Counselling, 28,* 21–39.

Tsang-Feign, C. (1993). *Self-help for foreigners: How to keep your life, family and career intact while living abroad.* Hong Kong: Asia 2000.

Woody, S. (1998, March/April). *Programming for reentry: Issues and solutions for study abroad returnees.* Retrieved March 8, 2007, from http://www.transitionsabroad.com/publications/magazine/9803/programming_for_reentry_from_study_abroad.shtml

Appendix A:
A Survey of International Students in the United States

SECTION A: Personal Information

Type of visa: _____ (e.g., F-1, J-1) Sex: _____ Age: _____
Where are you from? _____ (country of origin)
Campus location: _____ (state)
Campus setting:
____ Urban area or major city
____ Close to urban area or major city (less than 45-minute drive)
____ Small town
____ Rural

SECTION B: Undergraduate Psychology Students

Year: _____ (e.g., freshman, senior)
Major: _____
Are you planning to pursue a graduate degree?
___ If yes, in what program? _____
Where? ____ United States ____ home country ____ another country
___ If no, please proceed to SECTION B.1
Please indicate source of financing for studies (check all that apply)
____ Student worker (non-federal work study)
____ Family support
____ Personal funding
____ Tuition waiver
____ Partial tuition waiver
____ Government support from your home country

____ Scholarship from your home country
____ Other (please specify): _____
Reason(s) for pursuing a psychology undergraduate degree in the United States:

SECTION B.1: Career Plans of Undergraduate Psychology Students

What is your career orientation after graduation?
____ Work permanently in the United States
Reason(s): _____
____ Work temporarily in the United States and then return to my home country
Reason(s): _____
____ Return to and work permanently in my home country
Reason(s): _____
____ Return to and work permanently in another foreign country
Reason(s): _____
____ Work temporarily in another foreign country and then return to my home country
Reason(s): _____
____ Other (please specify): _____
Reason(s): _____

SECTION C: Graduate Psychology Students

Current graduate program: _____ (e.g., clinical, I/O, cognitive)
Where? ____ United States _____ other (please specify) _____
Degree seeking: ___ master's (terminal) ___ doctoral (PhD) ___ doctoral (PsyD)
Year in program: _____
In which academic discipline did you obtain your bachelor's degree?
_____
Where did you obtain your bachelor's degree?
___ home country ___ United States ___ another country
Are you receiving financial assistance? ____ Yes ____ No
If yes, what type of financial assistance?
____ Tuition waiver & monthly stipend
____ Partial tuition waiver & monthly stipend
____ Monthly stipend only
____ Fellowship
____ Government support from your home country
____ Scholarship outside of department/program
____ Other (please specify): _____
What type of assistantship position have you held? (Check all that apply)

____ Research assistant
____ Teaching assistant
____ Graduate assistant (administrative)
____ Other (please specify): _____
Do you currently have an internship in the United States?
___ Yes ____ No
____ Not required
Are you currently in a postdoctoral position in the United States
_____ Yes _____ No
If no, are you planning on applying for a postdoctoral position?
____ Yes ___ No
Reason(s) for pursuing a psychology graduate degree in the United States:
_____

Section C.1: Career Plans of Graduate Psychology Students

What is your career orientation after graduation?
_____Work permanently in the United States
Reason(s): _____
____ Work temporarily in the United States and then return to my home
country
Reason(s): _____
____ Return and work permanently in my home country
Reason(s): _____
____ Return and work permanently in another foreign country
Reason(s): _____
____ Work temporarily in another foreign country and then return to
my home country
Reason(s): _____
____ Other (please specify): _____
Reason(s): _____
What is your career goal?
____ Academic position in the United States (teaching and research)
____ Academic position in your home country (teaching and research)
Do you anticipate that you will require additional training in your home
country?
____ Yes ____ No
____ Academic position in the United States (teaching only)
____ Academic position in your home country (teaching only)
Do you anticipate that you will require additional training in your home
country?
____ Yes ____ No
____ Research position in the United States
____ Research position in your home country

Do you anticipate that you will require additional training in your home country?

____ Yes ____ No

____ Practice position in the United States

____ Practice position in your home country

Do you anticipate that you will require additional training in your home country?

____ Yes ____ No

____ Consultation position in the United States

____ Consultation position in your home country

Do you anticipate that you will require additional training in your home country?

____ Yes ____ No

____ Other (please specify): _____

Appendix B:
Additional Resources for International Students

Web Sites for International Students—Chapter 1

- EduPASS: http://www.edupass.org/immigration/
- EducationUSA: http://www.educationusa.state.gov/
- International Student Guide to the United States of America: http://www.internationalstudentguidetotheusa.com/

International Student Resources at Your University—Chapter 4

Bloom, D., Cohen, N., & Karp, J. (1998). *The PhD process: A student's guide to graduate school in the sciences*. New York: Oxford University Press.

Hayden, M., Thompson, J., & Levy, J. (Eds.). (2006). *The Sage handbook of research in international education*. Thousand Oaks, CA: Sage.

Hess, A., & Walfish, S. (Eds.). (2001). *Succeeding in graduate school: The career guide for psychology students*. Mahwah, NJ: Erlbaum.

McCulloch, G. (Ed.). (2007). *Encyclopedia of international education*. New York: Routledge.

Stevens, M., & Wedding, D. (2005). *PSYCHOLOGY: IUPsyS Global Resource* (CD-ROM). East Sussex, United Kingdom: Psychology Press. (The *Directory of Major Institutions for Psychological Research and Training* will be especially useful for international students.)

- http://www.nafsa.org/public_policy.sec/international_education_23—This Web site provides a list of current state-level initiatives that benefit international education at the postsecondary level, such as legislation, proclamations, consortiums, and commissions.
- http://opendoors.iienetwork.org—This helpful Web site provides a wealth of information for international students.
- http://www.am.org/iupsys/links.html—International Union of Psychological Science [IUPsyS]
- http://www.psychgrad.org—The Psychology Graduate Applicant's Portal
- http://www.appic.org—The Association of Psychology Postdoctoral and Internship Centers

Funding Resources for International Students— Chapter 5

- http://exchanges.state.gov/education/fulbright/commiss.htm (The Fulbright Program)
- The Fulbright Program: http://us.fulbrightonline.org
- http://www.globalexperiences.com/internships
- http://www.internationalstudentloan.com
- http://www.internationalscholarships.com
- http://www.cie.uci.edu/iop/internsh.html
- http://www.internationalstudent.com
- http://www.irex.org/programs/muskie
- http://www.fundingusstudy.org
- http://www.ecis.org/resources
- http://www.ewu.edu
- http://www.maldef.org/pdf/Scholarships_01252003.pdf
- http://hs.houstonisd.org/debakeyhs/Departments/counselors/Undocumented.html
- http://www.nygearup.org/collegesense/students/scholar_undoc.htm
- http://www.ccc.edu/financialaid/nonres_scholarship1.shtml
- http://www.finaid.org/otheraid/undocumented.phtml

- http://www.hacu.net (Hispanic Association of Colleges and Universities—Loans and scholarships)
- The American Association of University Women: http://www.aauw.org
- The American Psychological Association Education Directorate: http://www.apa.org/ed/graduate/homepage.html
- The American Psychological Association Women's Programs Office: http://www.apa.org/pi/wpo/fellows.html
- Bureau of Educational and Cultural Affairs of the U.S. Department of State: http://www.educationusa.state.gov
- College Board Scholarship Search: http://apps.collegeboard.com/cbsearch_ss/welcome.jsp
- Edupass: The Smart Student Guide to Studying in the USA: http://www.edupass.org
- Fastweb: http://www.fastweb.com
- Finaid: http://www.finaid.org
- The Foundation Center: http://www.fconline.fdncenter.org
- Global Student Loan Corporation (GSLC): http://www.globalslc.com
- Grantsnet: http://www.grantsnet.org
- Graduate and Postdoctoral Extramural Support (GRAPES) Database
- http://www.gdnet.ucla.edu
- The Hobsons U.S. Education Guides: http://www.USeduguides.com
- Institute of International Education: http://www.iie.org
- International Education Financial Aid: http://www.iefa.org
- International Student Guide: http://www.internationalstudentguidetotheusa.com/
- International Scholarships Search: http://www.internationalscholarships.com
- International Student Loan: http://www.internationalstudentloan.com
- National Science Foundation: http://www.nsf.gov/funding/
- Open Society Institute/Soros Foundations Network: http://www.soros.org/grants
- PITSCO's selections of grants and funding: http://www.pitsco.com/resources/grants.html
- Scholarship Resource Network Express: http://www.srnexpress.com
- U.S. Department of Education: http://www.studentaid.ed.gov
- United States Information Agency: http://www.usia.gov
- U.S. Network for Education Information: www.ed.gov/NLE/USNEI

Visa and Work Permit Information—Chapter 6

- http://www.unitedstatesvisas.gov
- http://travel.state.gov/visa/visa_1750.html

Resources on Culture in the United States—Chapter 7

About school and school-related issues:

- http://www.nafsa.org
- http://www.exchange.state.gov/education/educationusa

Cheap books:

- http://www.half.com
- http://www.textbooks.com
- http://www.amazon.com

Recreation:

- http://www.cityguides.com
- http://www.citysearch.com
- http://www.clubfreetime.com

Ethnic communities online:

- http://www.turkishny.com
- http://www.russianny.com
- http://www.indiaexpress.com
- http://www.nlpa.ws (the National Latina/o Psychological Association)

Travel sites:

- http://www.expedia.com
- http://www.travelocity.com
- http://www.amtrak.com
- http://www.greyhound.com

Other resources:

- U.S. Postal Service: http://www.usps.gov
- Information on used car prices: http://www.kbb.com
- Campus safety and personal security: http://campussafety.org/

Recommend Reading— Chapter 9

Gulgoz, S. (2001). Stresses and strategies for international students. In S. Walfish, & A. K. Hess, (Eds.), *Succeeding in graduate school: A career guide for psychology students.* Mahwah, NJ: Erlbaum.

Selected Online Teaching Resources—Chapter 10

- Office of Teaching Resources in Psychology Online: http://www.teachpsych.org or http://teachpsych.lemoyne.edu
- Michigan State University TA Program Resources: http://www.tap.msu.edu/nvgt/rescs/tap_res.html
- University of Hawaii Teaching Tips: http://honolulu.hawaii.edu/intranet/committees/FacDevCom/guidebk/teachtip/teachtip.html
- Center for Teaching Excellence at the University of Illinois Urbana–Champaign: http://www.oir.uiuc.edu/did/Resources/Illini%20Instructor/ITA_Communication.html
- The University of Northern Iowa Compendium of Online Resources, by Dr. Lida Walsh: http://www.uni.edu/walsh/teach.html
- University of California Berkeley Compendium of Suggestions for Teaching With Excellence: http://teaching.berkeley.edu/compendium/

Research Resources— Chapter 11

GENERAL RESOURCES

Black, T. R. (1999). *Doing quantitative research in the social sciences: An integrated approach to research design.* Thousand Oaks, CA: Sage.

Denzin, N. K., & Lincoln, Y. S. (2005). *Handbook of qualitative research.* Thousand Oaks, CA: Sage.

Greenfield, T. (2002). *Research methods for postgraduates.* New York: Cambridge University Press.

Gliner, J. A., & Morgan, G. A. (2000). *Research methods in applied settings: An integral approach to design and analysis.* Mahwah, NJ: Erlbaum.

Heppner, P. P., Wampold, B. E., & Kivlighan, D. M., Jr. (Eds.). (2008). *Research design in counseling* (3rd ed.). Belmont, CA: Thomson Brooks/Cole.

Locke, L. F., Spirduso, W. W., & Silverman, S. J. (2004). *Reading and understanding research.* Thousand Oaks, CA: Sage.

Smith, R. V. (1998). *Graduate research: A guide for students in the sciences.* Seattle: University of Washington Press.

THESES AND DISSERTATIONS

Dunleavy, P. (2003). *Authoring a PhD: How to plan, draft, write, and finish a doctoral thesis or dissertation.* New York: Palgrave Macmillan.

Glatthorn, A. A. (2005). *Writing the winning thesis or dissertation: A step by step guide.* Thousand Oaks, CA: Corwin Press.

Heppner, P. P., & Heppner, M. J. (2004). *Writing and publishing your thesis, dissertation, & research.* New York: Brooks/Cole and Wadsworth.

Mauch, J. E., & Park, N. (2003). *Guide to the successful thesis and dissertation: A handbook for students and faculty.* New York: Marcel Dekker.

Thomas, M. R., & Brubaker, D. L. (2000). *Theses and dissertations: A guide to planning, research and writing.* Westport, CT: Bergin and Garvey.

Thomas, M. R., & Brubaker, D. L. (2001). *Avoiding thesis and dissertation pitfalls: 61 cases of problems and solutions.* Westport, CT: Greenwood Press.

Wolcott, H. F. (2001). *Writing up qualitative research.* Thousand Oaks, CA: Sage.

RESEARCH ETHICS

Hersen, M., Michelson, L., & Bellack, A. S. (1984). *Issues in psychotherapy research.* New York: Plenum Press.

Elliott, D., & Stern, J. E. (1997). *Research ethics.* Hanover, NH: University Press of New England.

Shamoo, A. E., & Resnik, D. B. (2002). *Responsible conduct of research.* New York: Oxford University Press.

FUNDING RESEARCH

Brewer, E. W., Achilles, C. M., Fuhriman, J. R., & Hollingsworth, C. H. (2001). *Finding funding: Grantwriting from start to finish, including project management and internal use.* Thousand Oaks, CA: Sage.

Bloom, F. E., & Randolph, M. A. (1990). *Funding health sciences research: A strategy to restore balance.* Washington, DC: National Academy Press.

Hamel, A. V., Heiberger, M. M., & Vick, J. M. (2002). *The graduate school funding handbook.* Philadelphia: University of Pennsylvania Press.

WEB SITES

- American Psychological Association (APA) Research Funding Bulletin: http://www.apa.org/science/researchfunding.html
- American Psychological Association Graduate Students (APAGS) Practical Tips for Completing Your Psychology Dissertation: http://www.apa.org/apags/edtrain/dissertationtips.html
- Community of Science (COS) Funding Resource and Expertise Database: http://www.cos.com/
- Intute (free online service providing access to Web resources for education and research): http://www.intute.ac.uk/
- National Center for Research Resources (NCRR): http://www.ncrr.nih.gov/
- National Institute of Mental Health (NIMH) Research and Funding Information: http://www.nimh.nih.gov/researchfunding/index.cfm
- National Institutes of Health (NIH) Grants and Funding Opportunities: http://grants1.nih.gov/grants/index.cfm
- Qualitative Research Websites: http://www.nova.edu/ssss/QR/web.html
- Thesis and Dissertation Advisors—On Call (an international network of professors, instructors, authors, and editors who provide guidance, feedback, and partnership so you can meet deadlines and graduate on time): http://www.dissertationadvisors.com/

Recommended Reading on Internships in Psychology— Chapter 12

Williams-Nickelson, C., & Prinstein, M. (2005). *Internships in psychology: The APAGS workbook for writing successful applications and finding the right match.* Washington, DC: American Psychological Association.

Index

About the Editors

Nadia T. Hasan, MA, is a doctoral student in counseling psychology at The University of Akron in Ohio. She earned a bachelor's degree in psychology from the University of Florida in Gainesville in 2002 and a master's degree in psychology from the University of Akron in 2005. Ms. Hasan is the chair of the American Psychological Association of Graduate Students (2006–2009). She was the 2005 corecipient of the Outstanding Contribution to Scholarship on Race and Ethnicity award of the section on Ethnic and Racial Diversity in Division 17 (Society of Counseling Psychology) of the American Psychological Association. Her research interests include international students, multicultural issues in counseling, education and training, and culturally sensitive health care. Ms. Hasan has published in the *Journal of Counseling Psychology, The Counseling Psychologist,* and *Training and Education in Professional Psychology.*

Nadya A. Fouad, PhD, is a professor at the University of Wisconsin—Milwaukee and training director of the counseling psychology program. She is former chair of the Board of Educational Affairs of the American Psychological Association (APA). She is editor-elect of *The Counseling Psychologist* and was president of APA Division 17 (Society of Counseling Psychology) from 2000 to 2001. She serves on the editorial boards of the *Journal of Counseling Psychology, Journal of Vocational Behavior, Career Development Quarterly,* and the *Journal of Career Assessment.* She served as cochair (with Patricia Arredondo) of the writing team for APA's "Guidelines on Multicultural Education, Training, Research, Practice, and Organizational Change for Psychologists."

Carol Williams-Nickelson, PsyD, is a counseling psychologist and the associate executive director of the American Psychological Association of Graduate Students, at the American Psychological Association headquarters in Washington, DC, where she oversees operations for the organization as its chief executive. Dr. Williams-Nickelson has provided services in a variety of health care and forensic settings, including hospitals, long-term care facilities, residential treatment centers, community-based organizations, private practices, and counseling centers. Her professional interests, activities, and publications focus on student advocacy and development, training and supervision, legislative advocacy, leadership, professional development, and, in particular, women's issues and mentoring.